12 ROUNDS OF
MENTAL
CONDITIONING

US VS LIFE

"THE BIG FIGHT"

ELLIOT ALLEN

12 Rounds of Mental Conditioning: Us vs. Life "The Big Fight"

Published and Distributed by The Mental Conditioning Movement, Queens, New York

Book Coach – Robin Devonish
Cover Design – Muhammad Asif
Editing – Dana Ferguson and Pen Publish Profit, LLC
Interior Design – Istvan Szabo, Ifj., Fiverr / Sapphire Guardian International

ISBN: 978-0-9994307-2-9

Printed in the United States of America

ACKNOWLEDGMENTS

The journey of completing 12 Rounds of Mental Conditioning would not be complete without acknowledging my family.

My beautiful wife Michele, (**my light**) is truly the best person I can ask for to be in my corner.

My sons, Isiah and Aaron, you both inspire me to keep going even when I feel like I cannot continue.

My lovely Mom, Mary Allen, who is truly the foundation of every round I fight in life.

Thank you all for being in my corner!

DEDICATION

I dedicate this book to my late father, Charles Allen Jr., and my brother, Eric Allen Sr, who is no longer with us.

I will never forget those Saturdays when we watched boxing together and talked about life for countless hours. Every boxing analogy in this book comes from the cherished life lessons you both taught me. I will carry those lessons forever. I love and miss you both dearly. THANK YOU!

CONTENTS

INTRODUCTION
PRE-FIGHT PRESS CONFERENCE

We are guaranteed two things on this earth: the gift of life and the promise of death. Everything between these two events boils down to understanding that our mindset is the key to dictating the terms or type of life we want. The more we prepare our minds, the greater the chance of attaining a championship mindset, leading to victory in the fight against life.

Attaining our goals and reaching our destination is a fight that requires **hours, days, months, years**, and sometimes **decades** of mental training. The challenger opposing us in reaching our destination is called "LIFE." The pitfalls, setbacks, and stumbling blocks we face in pursuit of our goals all fall under the umbrella of "LIFE." Through conscious and intentional training, however, we can put ourselves in top mental shape to prepare for the fight against "LIFE."

The sport of boxing provides many examples of the twists and turns that fighters endure during a boxing match. There is a deep correlation between the fight we engage in with "LIFE" daily and the boxing matches in the ring. Over the next twelve rounds (chapters) of this book, we will see some parallels of how life plays out in a boxing match-up and make the comparison to our everyday fight.

The first and arguably most important key is learning how to train our minds. As we go through the next twelve rounds, we will,

1. Become equipped with various tools for training.
2. Establish a training foundation based on the four Principles of Mental Conditioning.
3. Reinforce the fundamental training methods explored in the first book of this series: "Mental Conditioning: Life's GPS."

Before we list the four Principles of Mental Conditioning, we must first define them. I suggest writing down these definitions and principles and keeping them near as you read.

And now, in the words of the late, great boxing referee Mills Lane, "LET'S GET IT ON!"

The definition of 'MENTAL CONDITIONING' is…

The strengthening of our minds to enhance our decision-making skills toward our big picture while staying the course.

What are the four Principles of Mental Conditioning?

1. Self-Evaluation.
2. Decision Making.
3. Big Picture.
4. Staying the Course.

With these *Principles* in hand, we are now ready to sound the bell to begin the training. Twelve rounds of mental training will build our endurance and strength in the fight against "LIFE."

Are you ready?

ROUND 1
DECIDING TO GET BETTER

Have you ever wondered what a fighter's thought process must be at the opening bell of the first round? The first round of a boxing match can set the tone for the rest of the fight. While many strategies are worked on during training and before the fight, the first two or three minutes of a first-round can determine how well those strategies and training are executed.

There are many questions the fighter will ask him or herself. A few of them are:

Am I in proper shape?

Did I run the extra mile needed for this victory?

Did I lift enough weights to make sure I was strong enough?

Did I spar enough rounds to ensure I am physically sharp with my boxing ability?

There are undoubtedly other questions a fighter will ask, but I believe that no question is more important than: "Do I want to get better?"

Certain people or opponents will provide you with the opportunity to get better. So, you must ask, "Do I want that challenge? Am I ready for this?" The reflex answer is, of course, I want to get better. However, it does take mental training to answer this question correctly.

> Why would a question that seems so trivial require training?

BOXING ANALOGY
EVANDER HOLYFIELD VS. MIKE TYSON

Champion boxer Evander Holyfield was trying to put together a fight with Mike Tyson. Due to various issues, there were difficulties in making that happen. Here were two highly celebrated heavyweight champions: Evander Holyfield, the world's current champion at the time. The other, Mike Tyson, was the former undisputed champion of the world and probably the most recognized fighter of his time.

*The rivalry brewed for years. Out of all the heavyweights, these fighters were the only two in the running for who was the best. To be the best, we must beat the best and be willing to take that challenge. For both fighters, this was an opportunity to "**get better**."*

When asked in an interview about the fight, Holyfield stated, "I have something he wants, if he really wants it." This struck me as a profound statement, particularly the last part: "...if he really wants it."

Why did Holyfield add that part? Well, a victory in the fight would give Tyson his title back and restore his status as the best heavyweight fighter in the world. A significant challenge would also make Tyson sharper than ever, ultimately allowing him to get better.

*So, the question again is, "Do you want to get better?" The truth is, we often ask this question in our personal lives regarding our growth. Deciding to get better requires mental strength and training. I would use the same statement Evander Holyfield used. Getting better is our life's challenge, which qualifies as something we want, "**if we really want it**!"*

Why would a question that seems so trivial require training?

Getting better comes with a price tag that's quite expensive. What did that cost mean to Mike Tyson? Tyson had lost the title of champion and some of his invincible aura with it. The notion of regaining both was attractive - but at what cost? This is where understanding mental strength comes in.

Let's look at the cost for Mike Tyson and bring it back to our everyday lives. Tyson had to give all he had physically to get in proper shape to beat Holyfield. Mentally, it takes significant commitment, hard work, and dedication to get in top physical shape. However, with all the tremendous hard work and commitment in training, was victory guaranteed? No! Was Tyson or anyone in his position willing to take that risk of hard work and not win the fight? This is when the question of deciding to get better becomes clearer. If Tyson hadn't taken the challenge, he still had his name and ability to make good money in boxing.

There is a word that plays heavily in this process - a word that opposes the decision to get better. That word is "**Contentment**"! It's a dangerous word in our efforts to move forward. Could Tyson have been content with where he was and still hold a pretty good status in the boxing world? He absolutely could have. Deciding to get better is expensive. If Tyson chose to get better by training extremely hard and lost the fight, not only would the result be physically damning but possibly mentally overwhelming and unrecoverable.

Let's look at how this becomes relevant to our everyday lives.

Foundational Statement:
The more prepared we are, the higher the cost of not being successful.

How does this concept of preparedness play in our decision to get better? We began the chapter by asking a trivial question: "Do I want to get better?" Now, we must establish a foundation to explore that question in more detail, specifically through the lens of "contentment" and when faced with the reality that "the more prepared we are, the higher the cost of not being successful." Why would someone be content with not getting better? During our *self-evaluation*, we constantly look at where we are in our lives. This, of course, takes great mental strength, along with two more important things to consider:

1. Survival.
2. Comfortable.

We often hear these words and equate them with being okay. This is not necessarily an inaccurate statement. This is what makes deciding to get better a mental challenge. Can we survive without getting better? Yes! However, getting better is a challenge to our mindset and progressive thinking in many ways. Survival can often be the ultimate goal of life. Remember, that does not mean we aren't eager to get better. Here is where we must pause and take another look at our Principles of Mental Conditioning, which are:

1. Self-Evaluation.
2. Decision Making.
3. Big Picture.
4. Staying the Course.

Which bin of our four principles can we store a survival mindset? It does not fit permanently in any of the principles of Mental Conditioning. This is an indication that survival is not building our mental muscle. Now, there are times in which survival is essential. This lends credence to the temporary placement of survival within our *Four Principles of Mental Conditioning.*

To "stay the course," sometimes survival is essential and temporarily falls within the "Self-evaluation" category. Survival is tricky because, naturally, we all want to. But the bigger, more critical question is whether we want to get better. If the answer is yes, then you realize a distinct difference requires much time in the *Mental Conditioning Gym™* to reveal your big picture.

Let's pause quickly to explain the all-important *Mental Conditioning Gym.* To build mental strength, it is imperative to have a place to work out. Much like a physical gym, we need a place dedicated to conditioning our minds. The location can be anywhere that we can genuinely think with no distractions. As we go through the rounds, we will establish the purpose and places we can use as our mental conditioning gym.

Getting back to survival, I will visit Evander Holyfield's response to Tyson wanting to fight him for the championship: "I have something he wants, if he really wants it." That challenge to Mike Tyson wasn't physical—it was mental. Does he want to survive? To be comfortable? To be content? Or does he decide to make the uncomfortable choice of returning to the gym and training for the challenge?

Let's spend some time exploring the differences between surviving versus getting better.

SURVIVING

Surviving is the most comfortable of the two terms. It's also the easiest. When we are put in a position to survive, we train our minds to continue doing what we have been doing. No matter the circumstances, we can adjust to being extremely comfortable staying in survival mode. Sometimes, in our lives, we have no choice but to go into survival mode—the ability to recognize *when* is part of getting better. To be clear, being in survival mode is not in and of itself a terrible thing. The actual process of building mental muscle is deciding to "*Get Out*" of survival mode. Remember - the rules do not change. The price of getting better is always more expensive.

GETTING BETTER

Deciding to get better after doing what you can to survive can feel overwhelmingly daunting. The good news is that we are already surviving. You can only go up from here! To get out of survival mode, we must be determined to focus on the thing that forced us into survival mode in the first place. Yes, that is scary. It most certainly will be mentally expensive. But you will find that getting out of the holding pattern is worth the price tag. It is worth it to *Get Better*.

BOXING ANALOGY

No fighter wants to get hurt in the ring. However, the reality is that 'Boxing' is a violent sport where punches are exchanged. A fighter is likely to get hurt by one of the punches absorbed. Getting injured during a boxing match can include loss of equilibrium, blurred vision, cuts to the eyes, heavy facial damage, broken hands as well as being knocked out. Let's pick one and match it up to our "survival" and "getting better" mentality.

We will use a boxer being cut from getting hit in the face. The cut occurs mostly just above the eye or on the eyelid. When the cut first happens, the blood will freely flow down and can run into the eye. Cuts can be controlled between rounds by the fighter's corner people who are there to give instructions and render aid to cuts if possible. Each boxing round is three minutes (two minutes if you are a female fighter). So, if the cut occurs one minute into the round, the fighter must survive the next two minutes before returning to their corner to work on the cut and control the bleeding. Does this require the fighter to fight differently than before the cut occurred? Possibly! In this particular case, survival options look like:

1. Grab.
2. Hold.
3. Run.
4. Cover the cut with their glove.

All are survival tactics. None of these are conducive to getting better and ultimately winning the fight. Hopefully, the corner people can do an excellent job on the cut and stop blood flow. If so, survival has been achieved - go for the win!

How much would that win cost, and are you willing to pay the price? The fighter is now expected to go out there in the next round doing the same thing that got them cut in the first place! The strategies being used were not necessarily ineffective. The fighter just got hit with a punch that opened up a cut. "LIFE" happens. Is that a risk? Is that an expensive price to pay to get better and ultimately win? Yes, and yes. The choice to get better puts the fighter at risk of being defeated but also sets them up for possible victory - because you never win until you try.

EMOTIONAL CONNECTION

Finding an intimate partner is truly one of the most challenging experiences in our lives. The journey is filled with plenty of peaks and valleys. But even in this real-life example, the question remains: Do you want to get better? Deciding to get better, coupled with the high emotion of dealing with a relationship, can be very mentally taxing. The principle of getting better through forward progress still holds true. Each relationship we experience, whether good or bad, allows us to get better.

However, the risk of getting stuck in survival mode still exists. Negative relationships can put us in survival mode. For example, if a boxer gets cut inside the ring, there can be good reasons to protect oneself temporarily. However, survival is up to the individual experiencing that perceived negative relationship. Some individuals never come out of that survival mode, resulting in them never opening their minds and hearts to another relationship again. When we decide to get better, what does that look like, and what is the cost? When an individual can, at some point, after a perceived negative relationship, put their mind and heart back into another relationship, that is a perfect sign of deciding to get better. Previous experiences, regardless of the outcome, always provide knowledge and wisdom. Knowledge and wisdom are critical tools for getting better.

Here is a question my dad always asked me: "How much is it?" It bears repeating—getting better is expensive. When you attach emotion to the price tag, the rate is further inflated, and taxes are higher than normal!

Emotional pain is often more painful than the physical pain we can experience. Living beings have built-in natural reflexes to retract from physical pain. Emotional pain is no different. So, imagine experiencing tremendous emotional pain, and to get better; we must put ourselves back in the same place to possibly experience that pain again. This requires immense hard work and dedication in the Mental Conditioning Gym. The good news is that this first round of deciding to get better will get us through the next eleven rounds. The challenging news is that each round must be fought as hard as possible, and each round's outcome must be evaluated honestly. This is something that you can only do.

ROUND 2
SELF-EVALUATION

Self-evaluation is the most critical component to training our minds to be successful and get wins in life. Another crucial word we will discuss in this chapter to accompany self-evaluation is "HONEST." Self-evaluation requires intense mental training just to be able to perform. Similar to Round One (deciding to get better), Round Two (self-evaluation) is fundamental to the training process. This foundational principle is essential to give us confidence when the fight against "LIFE" gets challenging. Self-evaluation is a mandatory exercise to strengthen our minds and must be performed daily as a prerequisite to all other exercises - including physical exercises. It can feel tedious, but it is crucial to building mental muscle.

Why do we need to do our self-evaluations? To be proficient at anything, it is imperative to understand *why* we do something. To go anywhere in life, we must have a starting point. When driving, we use GPS systems to navigate where we want to go. While it is necessary to type in the coordinates or details of where we want to go, it is equally, if not more, essential for the GPS to know where we are currently. We must know the starting location to go anywhere. If the starting location is inaccurate, we cannot complete the trip. Ultimately, we will never reach the final destination because the directions will be based on an inaccurate starting point. In this example, that starting location is the equivalent to our Self-evaluation.

So, what does that mean to our everyday lives? As we go through the decision-making process of our lives, it is essential to have an honest accounting of who we are and where we stand now. The place we are mentally today may not be where we were last year or even last week. The results of our self-evaluation are only sometimes what we want to admit to ourselves. No matter how mentally strong you are, this process is always challenging. By nature, we are driven to have positive thoughts and can easily block out or dismiss perceived negative thoughts. The experience of evaluating ourselves is very humbling, but that is precisely why it's necessary.

BOXING ANALOGY

Brian Adams
Decorated Golden Gloves Champion

As fighters go through a training camp preparing for a fight, evaluating themselves is equally, if not more important, than physical training. While fighters train to face an opponent, they must be clear about what their body can do on fight night. Many different things can occur that affect that Self-Evaluation. On fight night, honest self-evaluation, in many cases, is ultimately the deciding factor as to whether a fighter wins or loses. This is particularly challenging because world-class athletes, specifically boxers, need an egotistical opinion of themselves and their ability to perform at a high level. For fighters to admit to some form of inferiority about themselves is to go against the norm. Ironically, the fighters who can do this - recognize and realize the nature of their limitations - often become the most successful.

This is evident in boxer Brian Adams. Adams is a Golden Gloves champion and one of the most decorated amateurs in the sport's boxing history. After turning pro, he developed some major hand issues, which stunted the progress of his boxing career. Interestingly, when Adams spoke about his second to last fight, he zeroed in on how self-evaluation got him through. Before the fight, he knew that his hand was severely hurt and would render him unable to use it to its full, natural abilities. It's a brutal self-evaluation to reckon with. Remember the ego we talked about in Fighters? Adams spoke about the adjustments he knew he would have to make going into the fight strictly because of his self-evaluation. A fighter's hands are their most valuable tool in the ring. How they use them will determine the winner of a given contest. Adams knew his opponent well enough to know he could hit him anytime he wanted and cause damage. He never questioned his ability to hit his opponent a high volume of times frequently.

Now, here is where self-evaluation comes into play. Adams knew his hand physically would not allow him to deliver the shots without the pain being unbearable and possibly rendering him unable to continue. Adams determined he would have to use more movement and selective punching. This would prolong the fight and perhaps give his opponent more opportunities to win. Ultimately, his self-evaluation and decision-making skills allowed him to use that movement and selective punches to get a decisive victory.

The danger of a dishonest self-evaluation would have meant disaster for Adams. Sure, he could have said to himself, "Yes, I'm fine. There's no pain in my hand, and I can get through this match without any adjustments." However, due to the reality of the injury, a high *volume of punches thrown or landed could have meant an inevitable defeat for Adams.*

In this analogy, we learned some essential things. The most critical part is the word "honest." Self-evaluation is a tricky part of the Mental Conditioning process. In evaluating ourselves, we will, without exception, unveil things that we do not want to accept. It's hard enough to accept things from other people that we do not want to hear. Now imagine the difficulty in accepting things we don't want to be true about ourselves. Some of these things are near and dear to our existence or goals. For this reason, it makes the task of honest self-evaluation extremely challenging. But failing to evaluate ourselves honestly can mean all our work to build mental muscle is built on a false or weak foundation. We must know our current location to reach our goals and aspirations. Living beings have the tenacity to push forward even under adversity. Think about it - how many times has the deck seemed to be stacked against us, but we continue to persevere? The constant pushing, even when things seem bleak, puts tremendous pressure on our mental strength. However, that mental strength can be recovered, replenished, and restored through strong mental exercises. What is the one key component that makes recovery possible? Honest Self-evaluation. In cases where we march toward challenges comforted by false or inaccurate Self-evaluations, they lead to the genuine risk of being unable to recover mentally. This price is too heavy to pay.

Imagine going up a mountain you've convinced yourself is 300 feet when it's 30,000 feet. As you climb to 150 feet, feeling as if you cannot continue, the thought of being halfway there and believing that maybe you can even see the top of the mountain gives you renewed energy to push on. Yet as you reach the 300-foot mark, most likely experiencing supreme exhaustion, you realize the climb continues for 29,700 more feet. The consequences can be mentally devastating.

An honest assessment of where the mountaintop is needed. If there is no accurate evaluation, how will that impact the journey to the mountaintop? When it is realized that the mountain is truly 30,000 feet and that at 300 feet, the top is nowhere in sight, it is possible to give up mentally. Mentally giving up will harm one's physical motivation, resulting in the climber giving up on reaching the mountaintop and achieving their ultimate goal.

This is why Mental Conditioning is so powerful. Through proper and accurate Self-evaluations, we can discover that many of the answers we so desperately seek in our lives are already within our mindset. The challenge of training our minds results in asking, "Can I get out of the way of the thoughts that block my forward momentum and progress?"

Physical imprisonment is a form of punishment used to reprimand individuals. However, allowing negative thoughts to take over our mindset is a form of mental imprisonment we impose on ourselves. Dishonest self-evaluations fail us in successfully achieving our goals, and we have no one to blame but ourselves. Just think about all of the things that can cause the mind to fall into mental imprisonment. What do you think makes our minds prone to false or dishonest Self-evaluations? Time to introduce another keyword:

EMOTION!

The word "emotion" is weighty with power! I often think about what the most powerful force on earth could be. Is it a Mack truck barreling down a highway at 80 miles an hour? Is it a 747 traveling at speeds upwards of 500 mph? Is it a powerful crane that builds skyscrapers, ultimately changing a city's skyline? So many physical forces of power can easily overwhelm the strongest human being. Of all the previously mentioned examples, however, none represents the most potent and powerful force on the face of the earth... Our Emotions!

OUR EMOTIONS!

Put the book down right now and think about your emotions and where they have put you in your life. It's possible that even the request to put this book down made you feel something powerful. Emotions can cause an individual to say, "Hold on! I will put this book down when I'm ready, not when I'm told." How does this factor affect our all-important self-evaluations?

One of our most challenging emotional tests comes in the wake of our relationships. We truly grow from the multiple relationships we encounter during our lives. Those relationships - both past and present, positive and negative - make an everlasting impression in our lives, ultimately impacting our mindset and who we are. These factors contribute significantly to our self-evaluation process. The evaluation does not regard the person with whom the relationship was shared; it is strictly about holding a mirror up to ourselves because every personal relationship alters our previous self-evaluation.

What makes this difficult?

When performing our self-evaluation, the goal is to identify who we are so that we can make the best possible decisions for ourselves. Relationships are like punches thrown at a fighter in a boxing match. No matter what happens, the punch that is thrown affects the fighter. The effect is only sometimes harmful. That punch can have a positive impact on the fighter. The main point is that the *evaluation* must be made after that punch. Some of our relationships are tough punches. They can change who we are dramatically. That change is not something we can control. The key is to find a way to understand that change within us and use it to our advantage. Even if the circumstances result in a change that we perceive as a step backward, we must resolve to do an honest self-evaluation to see the silver lining.

The challenge can seem overwhelming, especially when your emotions are high. In that negative relationship that ended badly, you naturally feel bad that the person you trusted left you in this sticky position. It's an instinct to deny that person the satisfaction of outwardly affecting you in any way, creating an emotional tug-of-war. By having an honest *self-evaluation*, one eventually realizes that the growth they're experiencing is due to the person who negatively affected them in that relationship. Moving forward, their decision-making will be altered, ultimately adjusting to the experiences of that relationship. This can be mentally challenging! You must be able to separate your emotions towards the relationship to perform your honest self-evaluation to understand why. If you do not know why you are doing an exercise, when things become more challenging, you will inevitably quit. I say all this to share that even when battling your emotions and the residual feelings of that relationship, you can still focus on that honest self-evaluation because you understand where it will take you. Clarity is life's goal, and the self-evaluation process is a critical component.

ROUND 3

DECISION MAKING

I am often asked, "Is Mental Conditioning Positive Thinking?" My answer is no. Mental Conditioning is reality-based thinking. To understand reality-based thinking, we must have clarity. Clarity and reality-based thinking are essential components to the process of training our minds because they are both vital to the all-important exercise of:

DECISION MAKING

Clarity is a challenging part of life and forward progress. If you're driving in your car and it's raining extremely hard, it becomes difficult to see. You may be an excellent driver, but if the road in front of you is unclear, it isn't easy to make decisions behind the wheel. Our everyday lives are no different. This is why honest *self-evaluation* is so important. As we move into the decision-making process, clarity takes up some valuable space in this exercise.

What is our obstacle when deciding to determine our ability to move forward? Circumstances in life can sometimes make clarity seem almost impossible. But it IS possible, especially after diligent work in the Mental Conditioning Gym. Getting clarity in our lives typically takes place under less than favorable conditions. Remember earlier when we talked about driving in the rain? As that rain is coming down hard, heavy, and fast, you cannot see the extra warning signs that call out to you about looming, life-threatening situations. Through the heavy rain, you try to decide whether or not to change lanes, but because visibility is nil, you can easily hit another car or run off the road. This may seem like an extreme example, but the decision-making process of life is equally high stakes.

There is an old saying:

PRESSURE BUSTS PIPES!

Making decisions under pressure can burst our pipes of life. The decision-making process is not necessarily the most difficult challenge. The pressure of the circumstances in which we must make decisions makes things complicated and unclear. With proper mental training, the decision-making process is not easier, but it will become more apparent. So, the most powerful exercise we will utilize to build our decision-making skills is Self-evaluation. Honest evaluation brings clarity and puts us in a position to make decisions that will even surprise us at times. We also need to take this time to look at the circumstances of not making any self-evaluations and how that could affect our decision-making.

BOXING ANALOGY
Evander Holyfield vs. Mike Tyson
Continued

We discussed Mike Tyson versus Evander Holyfield in Round 1 (deciding to get better). We highlighted the mindset of deciding to get better in fighting each other. Holyfield defeated Tyson in their first fight in a very entertaining and competitive way. Holyfield was able to gain an advantage over Tyson with his first-class counterpunching. Tyson's biggest attribute is his authentic ability to deliver devastating knockout punches to his opponents. Tyson's opponents find it quite challenging to swing back under the pressure of him delivering powerful combinations. In the fight with Holyfield, Tyson found himself with an opponent who could swing back after Tyson's attack. Holyfield could do that effectively, resulting in victory in their first fight. When taking the rematch, I am sure Tyson appreciated Holyfield's skills. Tyson also noted Holyfield was intentionally clashing his head against Tyson's, which is illegal in a boxing match. The clash of heads did cause a cut to Tyson's eye in their first battle. He believed it was a critical factor in his defeat.

I saw a video clip of Tyson stating he always believed he was a superior man. Fighters must have that mentality. However, the decision-making process must involve mental modifications to clarify the self-evaluation. Tyson knew Holyfield's counterpunching skills were superior, which was the difference in the first fight. He also felt the tactics being used by Holyfield in clashing heads was a factor in the first fight. What adjustments did Tyson make to compensate? Tyson got himself in better physical shape after that initial loss to Holyfield. Would that be enough? There were no strategy changes to combat the counterpunching of Holyfield or the clashing of heads. Upon entering the ring that night, Tyson was in better shape, which he believed would carry him through. Once the fight started, however, he immediately realized that would not be the case. Holyfield's counterpunching once again proved to be a problem for Tyson that he could not answer. Again, in the second fight, a clash of heads opened up a nasty cut to Mike Tyson's eye.

So, let us ask a question. Why did Mike Tyson decide not to change some of his previous strategies to give himself a better chance to win? Were there things Tyson could have done to decrease the opportunities Holyfield had to counterpunch him and prevent the clash of heads? Of course, but it would require a major decision. It would require Tyson to concede that Holyfield's counter-punching ability was too great a deficit to overcome. Also, he would have to accept that the referee didn't see the clash of heads the way Tyson did, so he would have to figure out a way to offset that.

All this would have to be done with the ultimate understanding that defeat was possible if Tyson failed to make any changes. A big part of decision-making is how we deal with previous decisions. Before the fight started, there was great CLARITY in the questions that needed to be addressed. Even with clarity achieved, it is not a foregone conclusion that Tyson would or could change his strategy— not because of a lack of information or clarity, but because of a lack of honest Self-evaluation.

Is this decision-making process over? No, it has just begun. Tyson could still win the fight. Remember, he made the prudent decision to get himself in better shape and physically prepared for victory. Although it appears that the incorrect decision was made in training to avoid making tactical adjustments, it is still possible during the fight to make those adjustments. Tyson's ability and skill level are so high that he can adjust once the fight starts. That is a more pressing decision-making process and far more challenging to have desired results. Does Tyson decide to make that adjustment and try to win the fight, or does he give up? Many believe Tyson chose to give up by biting Holyfield's ear, breaking the rules, and, unfortunately, being disqualified. This example gives a powerful testimony to the importance of Tyson's lack of Self-evaluation and subsequent decision-making. This is a complex process. It requires lots of time in the Mental Conditioning Gym to have the mental strength to execute properly.

Decision-making is the most direct determinant of our life's journey. We make hundreds of decisions within the first few hours of being awake, dramatically impacting the rest of the day. Any decision on any given day can affect the rest of our lives.

Let's consider things through a short-term lens. The time we wake up in the morning is an important decision regarding when we will get out the door. If we have something scheduled, do we wake up extra early or snooze the alarm till the last minute? Can this impact our entire day? What are we going to wear? What time do we need to leave? Are we going to eat before leaving? If we eat, what are we going to eat? All these decisions can be made within the first 30 minutes of waking up. There are no wrong answers, but they are based on the individual, and each person must do their own Self-evaluation.

Honest Self-evaluation

Having a specific time to be somewhere sets the tone for our first decision of the day. Is it important to the individual to be on time?

Honest Self-evaluation

How long does it take us to get prepared after we wake up? If we decide to be on time, preparation is vital.

Honest Self-evaluation

What exactly are we going to wear? Depending on where we are going, what is appropriate?

While the decisions may appear trivial, each decision is exceptionally high value. Understanding this is an integral part of understanding Mental Conditioning. Every decision you make has a profound impact on the next decision. With these three factors alone, let's see how it affects the next 4-8 hours of the day. If being on time is important and we give it value and weight in our decision-making, we likely decide to get up at least one hour earlier than normal. There is an understanding that being late will put you under pressure to do what you have on deck that day. People often say, "I felt like I just couldn't catch up the whole day" (if they started late.) When you arrive at the destination, you feel behind.

On the other hand, some people thrive off of that "coming from behind" feeling. If they are on schedule, it may trigger boredom and cause them not to be as sharp.

Is there a correct answer for the appropriate time to get up? No, it's up to the individual. The individual can make the decision based on who they are. Most importantly, the impact of the decision must be understood. How long does it take to get prepared? For that person who knows running behind will affect the entire day, it is in their best interest to make a clear assessment of how long it takes to get ready. For that person, it takes one hour of preparation - maybe two. It's up to the individual to set the alarm clock with the appropriate two-hour cushion to get ready. It's also important not to hit the snooze button repeatedly when the alarm goes off.

I'm highlighting what takes place in a not-so-significant decision. However, it is a foundational decision that determines the fate of the rest of the day. How important is it to be honest with ourselves when making decisions? Can we afford to lose an opportunity by not getting to a place on time, or more importantly, being mentally on time once we reach said destination? We can arrive on time, but the stress of rushing to get there can make us mentally unprepared to do what is necessary to be successful, resulting in a missed opportunity.

Our decision-making skills determine how we attack life and the tasks ahead. We can blame circumstances, situations, and outside influences. However, it's an integral part of building mental conditioning to understand that, ultimately, our decision-making skills play a massive role in the direction of our lives. When you sit down in the Mental Conditioning Gym and analyze that reality, it's a very scary thought. Excuses are a significant "aid" in accepting things we fall short of in our lives. We must be careful about how we use the word "aid." Excuses are a "false aid." They represent a broken mental crutch - if you try to continue, you will undoubtedly fall at some point. Understanding the enormous strength behind enhanced decision-making skills puts us in a position to conquer "LIFE" even when it seems the odds are against us.

BOXING ANALOGY
SUGAR RAY LEONARD VS. MARVELOUS MARVIN HAGLER

Sugar Ray Leonard versus Marvelous Marvin Hagler was another highly anticipated fight fans desperately wanted to see in the sport's history. This scenario is interesting because so many high-stakes decisions went into this fight. Right after Leonard's monumental fight with Thomas Hearns, it seemed like the perfect time to make the fight with Hagler. One huge factor that weighed heavily on the fight was the fact that Leonard had suffered a severe eye injury as a result of the fight with Hearns. Due to a detached retina, he was being advised by his doctors never to fight again or else risk going blind. It was still anticipated that Leonard would go ahead with the fight with Hagler. The ball was somewhat in Leonard's court to make the fight happen. Hagler had clearly stated he would take the fight on any terms. Leonard had battled all the other starfighters of his division and came out on top. Hagler was the remaining chess piece that everybody wanted to see played. At this time, Sugar Ray was the cash cow of the sport. He generated an enormous amount of money in and out of the ring. Hagler was the blue-collar worker in and out of the ring. He also defeated all the other starfighters in the division. So, it came to a head! Hagler was on board, and now it was up to Leonard to say he wanted to agree to the fight. There was a huge press conference called for Leonard to announce his decision.

Let's set the scene: picture hundreds of people, including Hagler, packed in a hall with no space to move. Everyone waited with tremendous anticipation to hear Leonard's decision. You could hear a pin drop! To the crowd's dismay and Hagler's complete disappointment, Leonard announces that the fight will never happen and that he will retire. What a blow! With Leonard's competitive nature, I'm sure he wanted to fight Hagler. However, his Self-evaluation allowed him to make that tough decision to retire and not fight Hagler. That is Mental Conditioning working in high form. Not being overwhelmed by a desire to do something your heart is not truly into. I am sure the diagnosis regarding his eye also affected his decision.

The desire never went away for Leonard to fight Hagler. Sometimes we need to see and identify specific triggers to transform that desire into something we genuinely want and are willing to do what it takes to get it. About three years after making his retirement announcement, Leonard attended a fight between Hagler and John "The Beast" Mugabi. After watching the fight, the trigger was pressed. Leonard believed he could beat Hagler and his heart was in it to make the fight, so the fight was made. To be clear, it wasn't that Leonard did not believe he could beat Hagler three years before.

Everything we are speaking of here is Self-evaluation and aligning it with Decision Making.

Let's point out one more decision-making scenario between Leonard versus Hagler. Leonard worked extremely hard during the training camp to get in supreme shape. During training camp fighters practice their game plan and the tactics they intend to use on the night of the fight. They spar (box) with other fighters to sharpen skills and practice game plans. Leonard believed he could stand there and trade punches with the stronger Hagler. About two weeks away from the fight, during a sparring session, Leonard was hit with a powerful punch that nearly knocked him out. He was practicing his ability to stay in close and exchange punches. This devastating hard hit he took in practice made Leonard rethink his strategy. If a sparring partner nearly finished him in practice, certainly Hagler will be able to close him out with the knockout. Leonard decided to change his fight plan. Instead of standing before Hagler trading punches, he used his movement and angles to avoid trading punches with Hagler. That was ultimately the difference in the fight that would allow Leonard to squeeze out a slim victory (according to the judges). Leonard showed supreme Mental Conditioning. His ego could have forced him to say, "I'm sticking with the plan and will brawl it out. That hard punch absorbed in practice was nothing to think about."

Let us summarize the decisions made in this Boxing Analogy:

When the opportunity was first presented to Leonard to fight Hagler, he knew his heart was not into the sport to the level needed to take on a challenge like Hagler. That's a difficult self-evaluation because there was enormous pressure from the whole boxing world to see this fight. Certainly, the financial opportunity was there also. Everything on the surface pointed to him saying yes to fighting Hagler. However, he knew his desire to win and be the best, and through his evaluation, he determined mentally he wasn't where he needed to be. Had he taken the fight initially maybe he would not have been victorious. Maybe he would not have been mentally ready to endure the challenges he did to get the victory. Secondly, in training for the fight honest self-evaluation allowed him to realize the fight plan to brawl would have put him at risk. It would not give him the best opportunity to win. HONEST self-evaluation positions us to enhance our decision-making skills. The art of decision-making is critical to obtaining wins in our everyday lives. We are not in control of circumstances, however, our evaluation puts us in a position to make prudent decisions that lead to us being in the best possible positions in our lives. The process is not easy, but understanding the results allows us to see things through a reality-based lens. What is the most important factor of looking through a lens?

CLARITY!

ROUND 4
FORMULATING THE BIG PICTURE

The lens is one of the most important parts of photographing with a camera. If we are truly trying to capture a snapshot of a moment, we must first see it in the lens. The clearer we can see the image through the lens, the better we can capture the desired snapshot. We aim to obtain the best picture when we line up the camera and focus our lens. When done properly, that picture can take you back to the moment it was taken.

Have you ever looked at a picture and thought, "Wow, it feels like I'm there!" A photographer will tell you that it is not easy to capture a picture that makes you feel like you are literally where the scene took place. Experienced photographer Lumumba David films and photographs many of our events in the Mental Conditioning Movement®. I asked him about the aspects of creating a clear picture, as I believe it parallels life. As it pertains to the factors of taking a good picture, David told me the following:

√ Position of Subject (shot composition)
√ Lighting- proper exposure. (Not too light, not too dark)
√ Blurriness - adjust focus
√ Lens - Find the correct one

All of these factors contribute to making the picture clear. The process is not easy and requires much time and effort to get it right. When taking pictures and videos at any one of our events, I am always in awe of the amount of setup it takes David to bring the event to life by capturing priceless moments.

Formulating our Big Picture in life is no different. The process is not quick. Formulating a clear Big Picture requires hours, days, and years of mental exercises. In the previous rounds, we discussed ways to prepare for this process mentally. It is important to first decide to get better. To do that, we have to push toward something. That something is a "BIG PICTURE," and to march forward, we must be clear about what it is exactly. Our "BIG PICTURE" must be accurate.

In Round 2, we discussed *self-evaluations*. This is a big part of keeping the big picture in focus. We must clearly and accurately evaluate who we are and where we want to go.

Direction is essential to getting to places in our lives. When we live our lives without direction, we become stagnant. Stagnation is a major source of mental muscle loss. Lack of forward progress leads to feelings of depression and loss of confidence. One of our modern tools, becoming an irreplaceable part of our lives, is our GPS systems. It is a tool that allows us to go anywhere without getting lost or confused about how to get there. Its usefulness is immeasurable. However, as useful of a tool as the GPS is, if we don't know where we are or where our destination is, the GPS is useless!!

Formulating our Big Picture in life is imperative. Where do I want to go? Identifying our big picture is a prevailing component in our lives. It gives us an amazing ability to have clarity even when the picture of life is unclear or there are other critical obstacles in front of us.

BIG PICTURE
BOXING ANALOGY

Sometimes a fighter's focus and Big Picture before getting in the ring on fight night is more significant than the actual fight. Let us revisit the rivalry between Evander Holyfield and Mike Tyson. The fight between the two was many years in the making. The road had many twists and turns before they even stepped into the ring. One of the major twists was Mike Tyson's incarceration. Throughout that time Holyfield would continue to box. He lost the title at one point to Riddick Bowe, a formidable, undefeated heavyweight fighter who commanded respect for his ability in the ring. They eventually agreed to a rematch after Holyfield lost to him in the first fight. Holyfield made some changes to his corner for the rematch. He brought in one of the most prominent boxing trainers of all time, the late, great Emmanuel Steward. Steward was the architect of the world-famous Kronk Gym in Detroit, Michigan. Emmanuel was impressed with his work ethic during his preparation with Evander Holyfield. He spoke highly of the confidence Holyfield displayed, bordering on arrogance. The most glowing observation of his training camp with Holyfield was a statement about his focus on fighting Mike Tyson! That was Holyfield's Big Picture!

Think about what we stated about the Big Picture's potential for our success and forward progress. In this situation, Holyfield had lost his title to the man he was training for (Riddick Bowe). The fight would not be easy, and it didn't look good regarding the adjustments he could make to win the rematch.

Holyfield was the underdog. Mike Tyson was still incarcerated and there certainly was no guarantee he would fight again when he regained his freedom. Emmanuel Steward talked about how Holyfield focused daily on Mike Tyson! He would talk about Tyson as if that were the current opponent. Mentally, this is the takedown to any fighter. Lack of focus on the current opponent usually reflects looking past the opponent. In this case, the opponent was the current heavyweight champion of the world. However, Holyfield's clear understanding of his Big Picture was the driving force behind any opponent en route to his final destination. So, we are highlighting how the road may not be so clear to others, but the Big Picture is very vivid to the individual. Emmanuel Steward was working to get Holyfield ready for the biggest fight of his career then, and it was baffling to hear the frequent talk about fighting a different opponent who was not even currently active. There is no way that anyone except Evander Holyfield could understand. He defeated Riddick Bowe in a spectacular performance to regain the heavyweight title.

Holyfield understood that if he did not defeat Bowe or any other opponent, the opportunity to fight Tyson (his Big Picture) would be severely affected.

In our daily lives, many storms cloud our judgment and take us off the path we're meant to travel on. This is why training our minds to identify our Big Picture clearly and accurately is important. If we can do that, we can reroute ourselves off the detour and back onto the path of life with purpose and light.

A question that must be part of our daily mental workout regimen is, "What is your big picture?" Does it match your self-evaluation? If you match up the two, your decision-making will be vastly sharper. Everyone's Big Picture is different, but the effect of the driving force is the same when identified clearly. Consider the following analogy and how it relates to our relationships as well.

BOXING ANALOGY

JARAD ANDERSON VS. CHARLES MARTIN

Sometimes our Big Picture is different from the current road we are on, but the road we're on is an intricate and vital part of the journey. This was true with the young fighter Jared Anderson, and we saw it tested in his matchup against Charles Martin. In the lead-up to the fight, there was a clip of the Hall of Fame boxer Roy Jones Jr. talking to Anderson about the passion and drive fighters need in the ring to dictate their big picture. It plays a critical part in the success of their career. Anderson began to get very emotional during the exchange. He respected Roy Jones's immeasurable knowledge and idolized him as a fighter. However, he did not necessarily agree with Roy Jones's path of his big picture towards boxing. Roy Jones spoke passionately about understanding what it means to achieve greatness in a sport through hard work and dedication to the sport. Anderson explained that his big picture was his family. He clearly stated the well-being of his family is what drove him to the boxing ring. His family was his big picture, not a specific opponent or title.

*Now let's look at that. This differs from many of the boxing analogies we will hear of in this book. The majority of the fighters are driven by the challenge in front of them which is their opponent in the ring. However, Anderson is driven by his family, ensuring his family is cared for financially. He knew that boxing could provide that opportunity, therefore his big picture comes to light from a different angle. Can you be in the ring and drive forward as Roy Jones was imploring him to do by not having his opponent in front of him being his big picture? Can he endure those punches when he gets hit with a good shot? Can he endure the fatigue? Can he endure adversity in the ring without the **big picture of boxing** being at the forefront?*

We got a chance to see his big picture tested. During the fight with Charles Martin, a ring veteran, Anderson was tested. Here, a young fighter is going against a skillful, experienced fighter. This scenario is always a great test for a young fighter, and this proved to be no different. Anderson started as expected with the youthful energy to give Martin great trouble. Martin was able to analyze things that he could take advantage of, and he was able to land hard shots on Anderson.

Now is when the big picture is tested. Martin was able to hurt Anderson. When you are hurt, only your big picture will allow you to continue to march forward and try to win. Anderson passed the test and dealt with the adversity of being hurt. He was challenged and came back for victory. Often, a young fighter gets badly hurt and that pain causes confusion. In the wake of that pain, there is a possibility that they give up trying, especially if the big picture is not at the forefront for victory. This fight greatly illustrates why the big picture is especially important. After being hurt, Anderson could "reset" himself and channel his energies for the win.

RELATIONSHIPS:

Relationships invoke some of the most intense emotions in our lives. They can be a driving force in the big picture or a major source of confusion. Falsely identifying our big picture can cause a lot of conflict and confusion. Let's examine both possible occurrences and the effects of both scenarios.

If we can properly identify our relationships as our life's big picture, it provides great direction. The key here is to properly identify it using a skill we constantly employ: self-evaluation. As we mature and grow in life, we begin evaluating and eliminating. We constantly evolve, and some things that once mattered are no longer essential. Unfortunately, we are creatures of habit and habits can be difficult to break. When we establish our relationships as the big picture in our lives, it requires constant re-evaluation. There will be occurrences in which evolution will reveal that a relationship is no longer conducive to the forward progress of our life. Now is when it is essential to understand the process of breaking a bad habit. It's important to see the damage of a bad habit: it can stunt growth or limit our progress. All the work we put into identifying our big picture as a driving force to our life success will be set aside. Traveling life's journey toward a false big picture is just as devastating if not more so, than having no big picture. Some effects of this include:

- √ Depression
- √ Total Lack of Motivation
- √ Low Energy Levels
- √ Constant Frustration
- √ Inaccurate Self Evaluations
- √ Behavioral Inconsistencies
- √ No sense of accomplishment, regardless of wins in life

What happens when we can match up our big picture with our relationships? It can put us in positions to do things we never thought possible. It gives us the power to deal with powerful forces such as our dislikes, fears, and insecurities. When we have a partner who is truly our big picture, our life's destination coordinates are extremely clear. Motivation to achieve our life's goals and purposes by matching our big picture with a relationship can result in:

√ Highly Motivated
√ Constant Energy
√ Refreshed Sense of Purpose
√ High Level of Focus
√ Prevailing Confidence in Pursuing Goals
√ Focused Self-Evaluations
√ Clear boundaries and parameters of life

All listed factors become somewhat of a natural part of our everyday lives and the confidence boost has a positive impact. We underestimate how important our energy levels are to our mental state. If our big picture clicks in line with our goals, we feel like we can keep going on with endless energy to do whatever is necessary to reach our desired life destination.

A fact that I would like to close on here as being important is establishing boundaries and parameters of life. We all have boundaries and parameters to stay within to get wins in life. While it is important to identify the limits of our boundaries, the most challenging part is staying within those limits. There is something we all know called willpower. Willpower is the ability to control one's actions, emotions, or urges. Even with strong willpower, we still need something to stand on and help control those factors. Establishing a good foundation regarding our boundaries and parameters is important, particularly in relationships. Certain behaviors, while enjoyable to an individual, are not at all conducive to being in a relationship. That type of matchup can pave the way for clarity in the decision-making process even when tempted by temporary pleasures that are not helpful to our big picture. We have experienced change in ourselves or witnessed changes in others individuals due to effects of a relationship. We must be careful to properly identify our big picture to ensure those changes are for the better and conducive to who we are, allowing us to do things we never thought possible. As we establish our parameters and boundaries, they will continually be challenged because life is forever evolving. This emphasizes why our big picture is overwhelmingly important.

ROUND 5
THE OPPONENT (LIFE) WON'T STAND STILL!

All the work we have put in so far, and all the work we have yet to put into the upcoming rounds is all in preparation for that most formidable opponent called "LIFE"! "LIFE" is always in shape, hits hard, and causes a very high level of damage to our mindset when it lands a hit on us. "LIFE" shows no mercy to its opponents. Therefore, preparation is our most valuable tool in the fight against "LIFE." We must prepare our minds to deal with whatever "LIFE" throws our way.

In the boxing ring, the trickiest thing to deal with is a fighter with tremendous versatility, one that is agile and moves quickly. So, let's look closer at the attributes of the opponent called "LIFE:"

1. VERSATILE.
2. PUNCHES YOU HARD.
3. FAST MOVING.
4. CONSTANTLY MOVING.
5. UNPREDICTABLE.
6. GREAT ENDURANCE.
7. NEVER STOPS PURSUING YOU.

These characteristics that make up an outstanding boxer are the same challenges that "LIFE" presents daily. How do these challenges specifically present themselves as constant opponents in our lives?

1 – VERSATILE – "LIFE" can adjust to any situation. So many times when we believe that we have found the answer to a life problem, "LIFE" readjusts and causes either another problem or a variation of the same problem you believed you had solved. When you think you've got "LIFE" cornered, watch out! The opponent will spin right out and catch you with a punch on the chin. Speaking of punches...

2 – PUNCHES YOU VERY HARD – How hard you get hit with punches is a big determining factor of whether or not we can continue, and if we do (if we are able), what does that look like? We know that "LIFE" punches extremely hard. Now couple that with "LIFE" having great versatility. That versatility allows "LIFE" to get in the perfect position to land its heaviest punches. Heavy punches increase the possibility of a devastating knockout situation. Think about times in our lives when we got hurt by a situation. Now envision how the two earlier attributes fit. Part of landing a sharp punch is positioning. What is our position in life at the given moment?

3 – FAST MOVING – An old saying quotes, "Life stands still for no one." It is absolutely true! "LIFE" is a never-stopping, fast-evolving opponent. We covered *decision-making* in Round 3, one of the most vital parts of Mental Conditioning. The swiftness of "LIFE" sometimes makes making decisions within the most efficient time limit difficult. This is when the speed of "LIFE" can easily overwhelm us. I ask you to reflect on times in your life and circumstances in which you felt overwhelmed. Many of us would say being put in more than one particularly challenging situation simultaneously can make things feel overwhelming. We may think if the challenges can come at a slow measured pace, we can take our time and make measured decisions. Unfortunately for us, "LIFE" is fast. So, we don't always have the option of taking our time and making slow precise decisions. We must therefore train our minds accordingly.

4 – CONSTANTLY MOVING – In the sport of boxing, timing is a critical part of establishing success in what you do. "LIFE" has an identical formula. Timing is everything and how we time our punches and movement dictates if we will get hit, or the force in which we take a punch. The challenge is trying to time a constantly moving target. "LIFE" is constantly moving, so those decisions are not easy to make. In the ring big punches need a target to be there to get hit. Even though a fighter can punch extremely hard, they have to be able to hit their opponent. In the fight against "LIFE" we certainly are trying to land our fair share of punches to win. The more we work on our mental strength the harder we can hit. Training is everything.

From a defensive standpoint, we must guard against "LIFE" constantly trying to hit us. "LIFE never stands still, so avoiding punches and landing punches are equally challenging. Constant movement can result in mental, physical, and emotional fatigue. When we are mentally exhausted, it greatly affects our decision-making abilities.

What does all this look like in terms of our everyday lives? We face hundreds, if not thousands, of decisions during our day. The magnitude of those decisions varies. The time allotted to make those decisions also varies; however, the abundance of decisions we have to make does not diminish. In some situations, our decisions will take considerable time. Even with that being the case, making more decisions is continuous.

EXAMPLE:

A major decision we face in life is whether or not to pursue certain relationships. When we meet a person, maybe we are at a stage where we are looking to settle down in a meaningful relationship that leads to possible marriage. This is a life-changing decision when you have a good candidate. Some things may hold you back, and making that decision will not be easy. Maybe the person is a smoker, drinker, or something else you are adamantly against. However, the individual has all the other qualities you seek.

You have a major decision to make. This is a normal process in the fight with "LIFE." "LIFE" never stops regardless of how many decisions are pending for yourself. It is possible that while figuring out how to move forward in this relationship you can be offered a life-changing job opportunity. "LIFE" is constantly moving! In an ideal world, we want to make a decision on our relationship and then be faced with deciding on our career after. This is a compounding situation in which both decisions are intertwined and affect each other, even though we have not decided on either question. With both of these life altering decisions pending, surely we will not be put in a position to make any other high magnitude decisions at this time. Unfortunately, that is not true. With both of those complex decisions on the table, the phone can ring and now you have to deal with some news of an aging relative being diagnosed with a life-ending disease. Again, another life-altering decision that is on the table. "LIFE" is constantly moving!

So how do we train for this?

One of the strategies used to prepare for an opponent in the boxing ring is to watch the film and study an opponent's tendencies. When facing a constantly moving opponent, it isn't easy to pick up a lot from just watching the film. You can see the opponent ("LIFE") will be moving, but the timing of that movement is impossible to pick up until you are in the actual situation. When there is constant movement, it is incredibly challenging to predict a rhythm. Speaking of being unpredictable....

5- UNPREDICTABLE – "LIFE" is about rhythm. When we have a dance partner, it is extremely important to dance and move in rhythm. Unpredictable movements from your dance partner can make it difficult to move in synchrony.

So, what does synchrony or good rhythm look like in our everyday lives? When we can make sound decisions that match our Self-Evaluation, it results in a good life rhythm. As individuals, we operate in a pattern of comfortability when we can have an honest Self-evaluation. Make no mistake, that comfort does not mean ease or lack of risk. We are willing to take on challenges that may seem beyond our reach because we are moving in our life's rhythm. The rhythm gives us the confidence to do things even when they're highly difficult.

Unfortunately, our opponent called "LIFE" is very unpredictable. Are there times when we have a dance partner or boxing opponent so unpredictable that it throws off our rhythm and cadence, shaking our confidence to move forward and execute? There are many times when that will be the case. My mother's favorite television show is Dancing With The Stars. It is a dance competition show where well-known people (who are not professional dancers) partner up with professional dancers to see which couple can best come together. The amateur dancers are unpredictable, so the amateur that can become the least unpredictable and get the best rhythm with their partner will ultimately look the best and win.

Boxing is a fitting example to highlight the problems unpredictability can cause in life.

BOXING ANALOGY

Floyd Mayweather, Jr.

Floyd Mayweather Jr. is undoubtedly one of the top fighters of his era, if not the best. Mayweather's career ended with him being undefeated in fifty professional fights. What is more impressive is that he had little trouble in the ring during those 50 fights. Not only did he go undefeated, but he also rarely ever lost rounds. The overwhelming majority of fights were won without doubt of the results. Mayweather's skill level was legendary for all eras of boxing. Mayweather liked to boast that he had mastered the game of boxing. He spoke of knowing what his opponents would do even before they did it. That ability afforded him the luxury of being able to fight in rhythm. When a fighter is fighting in rhythm it isn't easy to contend with them. Their confidence level makes difficult tasks in the ring look extremely easy. Throughout Mayweather's career many highly skilled fighters challenged him. Unfortunately, for his opponents, his skill level was unmatched. Mayweather consistently made it clear he was superior.

However, two opponents in particular did stand out as giving Mayweather trouble in a fight. Ironically neither guy was a highly skilled boxer. Both fighters had very unorthodox styles. Unorthodox styles in the boxing ring make for a very unpredictable fighter. The two fighters were Emanuel Augustus and Marcos Maidana. They did not throw punches from traditional boxing stances. Under normal circumstances, following a fight pattern like this is not recommended. However, in this particular case, these two fighters were able to disrupt the rhythm of the great Floyd Mayweather Jr. Mayweather is normally the defense expert and very proficient at avoiding punches during his fights. In both fights, we saw him get hit more than usual. You would think it was a skill, but the unpredictability caused Mayweather so much trouble. He had to fight Maidana a second time because the first fight had a close decision. The rhythm of a fighter dictates so much of the fight. These two fighters were able to interrupt the almost impenetrable rhythm of Mayweather. They could not defeat him, but their unorthodox styles made Mayweather uncomfortable in the ring which was a rarity.

While writing this example, I am reminded of the advice the great trainer Teddy Atlas gave Michael Moorer during his first fight with Evander Holyfield. He used the analogy of an old car (the old car being Holyfield). He told him that letting the old car go downhill will make it. Going downhill it stays in rhythm. If you make that old car go up the hill, it will not make it. So, Atlas told Moorer to make Holyfield fight like he was going up the hill so he would get out of rhythm and crash. You do that by being unpredictable and changing the pace.

Think about this: even when walking, if we stay at the same pace, we can walk for long periods. However, if you walk at different paces, you will quickly wear out your energy (and the soles of your shoes).

The challenges and questions "LIFE" sends our way constantly throws us off our rhythm in our everyday lives. How often have we self-evaluated and felt like, "Yeah, I'm in a good place!" Things are flowing just as you want it. The growth is moving at the steady pace that works for you. You are working at a job with which you are happy. You find you have endless energy even though you may be working many hours. You are in rhythm! Suddenly, "LIFE" can swing at you and hit you hard. Perhaps your position at the job becomes unstable. What does that look like? It can vary. It could be something as simple as a new person on your job or someone you have to deal with in your business. This person can turn your life rhythm on its head. Ironically, you may start working fewer hours but find yourself more fatigued. That's just an illustration of how the rhythm of "LIFE" can significantly affect how you physically feel.

Sometimes things we perceive as good things can greatly impact our rhythm. Earning more money is not a terrible thing. However, as the old saying goes, "More money, more problems." We have a routine of managing our money even when it is tight, and often we get used to that. A dramatic increase in money requires adjustments. If we don't make a concerted effort to do that, we become mentally exhausted dealing with something we always wanted. We must condition our minds to be ready for the unpredictable. That conditioning will increase our mental endurance.

Speaking of Endurance:

6 – GREAT ENDURANCE – As the opponent called "LIFE" keeps moving, believing that "LIFE" will slow down is a natural line of thinking. Unfortunately, that would be a dangerous mistake. "LIFE" has an inhuman endurance that never slows down or gets tired. No matter the situation, "LIFE" will continue putting pressure on us. How often have you asked, "How much more can I take?" Despite us feeling that way, "LIFE" will continue to deliver the blows. Think about the terms "giving up" or "quit." Is that a physical or mental term? Can our bodies fail us to the point we cannot continue? Sure, that is possible. However, giving up and quitting is more of a mental submission.

What makes us mentally give up or quit? Often, it is the mindset where we see no possibility of winning. When in a battle, we evaluate our opponents along with ourselves. We can feel when we are mentally drained. When "LIFE" pushes back on us, it's difficult not to give up and quit. This does not necessarily reflect what one can do physically and our ability to execute. It is about having the willpower to stay on course even when we feel mentally exhausted, even when we know our opponent "LIFE" will never run short on endurance. It becomes a very frustrating situation since the determining factor of whether or not to give up is based on our mental endurance.

BOXING ANALOGY
MIKE TYSON VS. DANNY WILLIAMS

In Mike Tyson's final competitive professional fight, he faced off against a lightly regarded opponent named Danny Williams. There was nothing in William's skillset that could pose a challenge to Mike Tyson. Even though Tyson was way past the prime of his career, it was apparent his skill level was superior to Williams. As the fight began there was no indication of anything being different from what was predicted. Tyson came out with his usual aggression and just as any typical Tyson opponent, Williams appeared to have a great deal of trouble managing the pressure. Tyson landed exceptionally good shots to the head and body.

But there was one X-factor here. At this point in Tyson's career, it was believed that being able to withstand the pressure early on would result in Tyson's endurance running empty. So, staying with the game plan, Williams withstood the pressure and extremely heavy punches landed by Tyson early. Inevitably, Tyson did indeed run low on endurance. Williams began to attack Tyson and land punches. The ending result was Williams forcing Tyson not to continue. Tyson eventually went down from a barrage of punches but was not hurt to the point that he could not continue. Instead, he decided to sit on the canvas and not get up. He knew his physical endurance was shot and his opponent had more energy. This resulted in Tyson's mental endurance failing and subsequently resulting in him quitting under those circumstances.

It was a powerful image to see Tyson sitting on the canvas with a clear head and mentally deciding not to get up. After the fight, Tyson announced his retirement because he knew this level of opponent should not even be competitive with him. This was an outstandingly HONEST Self-Evaluation. While not an easy one and in some aspects, very tough to observe, Tyson's decision to sit on the canvas as the referee counted him out showed his mental growth.

7 – NEVER STOPS PURSUING YOU – The main factor of Williams defeating Tyson was his never relenting his pursuit of Tyson once he knew his endurance was key. We can use many tactics to push past our lack of mental endurance. We know for sure that "LIFE" is never going to run out of endurance. So, although that's quite a daunting prospect to think of, it's useful information to be aware of in our fight against "LIFE." We must consider what "giving up" and "quitting" mean in specific situations. Sometimes not firing back at "LIFE" can be the answer. This does not constitute "giving up" or "quitting." It can allow you to rebuild and restore endurance, which allows you to endure hits from "LIFE" because it never stops pursuing. This is why it is important to build mental muscle. Using the four principles of mental conditioning, we must implement *self-evaluation* and the big picture to stay the course, even when our endurance is low. It's important to fight the temptation to feel overwhelmed. We must stand on the confidence of our work in the Mental Conditioning Gym. These exercises and principles are things we train to prepare us for the fight with "LIFE."

ROUND 6

LEARNING DURING THE FIGHT

We have learned that "LIFE" doesn't stand still. So, our fight with "LIFE" is constantly in progress. All the factors we discussed in the previous rounds are tools we can use during the fight. Even though we have these tools, we have to learn when to apply them and the principles we can use to apply the tools. This all must be done during the fight.

The majority of the time there will be no break in the action. We get a few minutes of rest between rounds, but the bell rings quickly, and we must answer the call. Throughout these first five rounds, we consistently mention building our mental conditioning. At this point I'm sure you're asking, "How?"

In this round we're going to learn how to build Mental Muscle. The process of learning to build mental muscle happens while we fight against ""LIFE." Some of what we will learn in this round is not parallel to boxing analogies. In boxing, fighters have 6-7 weeks or longer of training before the big fight. In our fight against "LIFE," that is not always an option. However, we can set the foundation from which we will be learning and subsequently building mental muscle. I like to call this foundation the Four Principles of Mental Conditioning. These principles are the building blocks that will allow us to learn while we are in the fight. Let's look at both and start building mental muscle from there.

MENTAL CONDITIONING DEFINITION

"The strengthening of our minds to enhance our decision-making skills toward our big picture while staying the course."

An essential part of building physical muscle +is repetition. One of the difficult parts of physical training is doing things repeatedly. Building Mental Muscle is not exempt from having to do things repeatedly. One of the exercises is just to read something numerous times. In some cases, we may need to write it over and over. Within this book, we purposely keep mentioning certain terms. It may seem redundant but that is how we build muscle. Training our minds has multiple layers. Each layer is challenging. The first step to absorbing the mental conditioning definition is reading it constantly. Writing it down is also good, so let's do it now.

REPETITION:

"THE STRENGTHENING OF OUR MINDS TO ENHANCE OUR DECISION-MAKING SKILLS TOWARD OUR BIG PICTURE WHILE STAYING THE COURSE."

The more you read the definition, the more you understand it. As you understand the definition, you can apply it to your fight against "LIFE." Applying the definition allows you to "Learn During The Fight." As "LIFE" hits us with different punches (challenges), the mental conditioning definition gives us the skills to navigate and solve those challenges while they happen in real time!

We further break down the definition of Mental Conditioning by implementing the associated principles. Same rules of repetition apply here. The more you read and write the Four Principles, the easier it becomes to apply them to fight against "LIFE." So specifically, how do we learn during the fight using the mental conditioning definition and principles? We first do an honest "self-evaluation" (Round 2). This allows us to learn about ourselves and where we are during a fight. We must understand and accept that the circumstances of the active fight with "LIFE" constantly alter the results of our self-evaluation (Round 2). This is key for us to learn what we can and cannot do during the fight. These adjustments must be made in real time and no matter the circumstances in the fight with "LIFE." At times "LIFE" will deal us numerous punches which can be overwhelming. We still have to be conscious of self-evaluating (Round 2) during the heavy punches. This is what makes learning during the fight extremely difficult.

BOXING ANALOGY
Muhammad Ali vs. George Foreman

Muhammad Ali boxed George Foreman for the Heavyweight Championship in 1974. Ali was already an established fighting Icon in the sport at the time. Foreman was a young, brash, hard-hitting champion who invoked fear in all his opponents. Foreman's punching power was legendary - a status still held in high regard almost 50 years later! Many feared for Ali who was starting to become an aging fighter at this point in his career. How could he withstand the punching power of the younger fighter, knocking fighters out, that Ali had trouble beating? Although there was great concern from boxing insiders and the public, Ali was supremely confident in his mindset. He knew he could beat Foreman. As the fight began, Ali used outstanding movement, foot speed, and fast hands to handle the onslaught of the stronger Foreman. Ali had an outstanding first round, establishing that he had the ability, movement, and hand speed to put himself in position to beat the champion. However, after the fight, Ali stated that even though he had a successful first round he learned he would not be able to continue doing the things he did throughout that opening round. Although his movement was effective, he evaluated that he was having to take two steps for every one step Foreman was taking. He also recognized that he was throwing far more punches than Foreman. These factors meant he knew he could not sustain that level fighting against a younger, stronger Foreman.

This is where the infamous "Rope-A-Dope" strategy was born. Ali would lean on the ropes with his hands up high to block Foreman's punches, but still allowed him to throw punches at him continuously. This solved the problem of too much movement and high volume of punches in this particular fight. Although the risk of getting hit with huge Foreman punches was a dangerous threat, Ali learned it was more efficient than continuing the constant movement that would have depleted his physical stamina. This is a particularly good example of Learning During The Fight. He was able to make the self-evaluation (Round 2) and make the adjustment (Learning During The Fight). Ultimately it proved to be the correct adjustment. Ali's strategy of enticing Foreman to throw a high volume of punches depleted the champion's endurance. Ali turned up his punch volume again in round eight and knocked George Foreman out with a sizzling combination of punches. Through "Learning During The Fight," Muhammad Ali won the match and regained the Heavyweight Championship of The World title in an stunning upset!

Let's look at how we apply this to our everyday lives. As different situations arise, there are lessons to be learned. What prevents us from learning while we are in the middle of these situations? One word: "EMOTIONS."

> "THE MOST POWERFUL FORCE ON THE
> FACE OF THIS EARTH IS OUR EMOTIONS!"

When we are in the middle of a difficult challenge in life, our emotions run high. Circumstances are stressful and we want the outcome to be in our favor. The higher the situation's stakes, the higher our emotions will be. As a result, everything stops. We cease to pivot from the path we're on by doing something different. We fail to "Learn During The Fight."

It is important to train our minds to "Learn During The Fight." It is a major factor in maintaining healthy connections in our relationships. Sometimes people readily admit they are in a toxic relationship, and "Learning During The Fight" is an excellent defense to the toxicity. How many times have we been involved in a situation in which we are continuously mistreated over and over? The first time was a shock and unexpected. The second time, perhaps a second chance will be given. By the third, fourth and fifth time, we must look within ourselves and admit we are not "Learning During The Fight." We ask ourselves questions like how does this keep happening to me? First and foremost, we must deal with the emotion of admitting things to ourselves that are not favorable. This is ultimately another illustration of why "self-evaluation" (Round 2) is so important to the process of Mental Conditioning. Self-evaluation lets you know you are making decisions not conducive to your forward growth. Emotions can stop our decision making (Round 3) process, resulting in a failure to learn during the fight against "LIFE."

Let us use a business example to highlight "Learning During The Fight." As we start our journey of working to earn a living as a young professional, there are some major decisions we have to make. For example, do we want to be an entrepreneur, or do we want to work for a company? There is no wrong answer. When we start working, we cannot fully answer these questions. At a young age with no experience, there may not be enough life information or experience to answer this question properly. Once the journey of working to earn a living starts, there is a good chance that there will be no real breaks to sit and assess for long periods without working. An individual may initially decide, "Hey I don't want to work for anyone." The decision can be made to go the route of earning a living through your own business venture. Consequently, an assessment will have to be made. After numerous years of trying to start a business, individuals may realize they cannot do it. The process of making an established business successful as an employee is one thing, but the struggle to even start a business as an individual is something else altogether.

Quick Chart Breakdown:

SELF-EVALUATION (ROUND 2):

Why is the individual struggling to start the business?
Remember Emotions stunt our ability to Self-Evaluate
A great deal of emotion goes into starting your own business!

EVALUATION:

Individuals may not want to embrace ownership of all situations fully. At startup, all phone calls need to be addressed by the individual. EVERYTHING MUST BE DONE BY YOU. The reality is that some of us don't want that responsibility. That is okay as long as we can evaluate that in ourselves.

This is a very real thing that can happen. Does this make the individual a bad person or wrong for displaying this behavior? No, but now we can talk about learning during the fight. One would have to learn from these factors and decide about being an entrepreneur during the all-important time of figuring out what they want to do. Financial stress is heavily involved in the fight. The emotion of wanting to be an entrepreneur is also heavily involved in the fight. What would be the thought process if the business is not producing as it should, largely due to the previously stated factors? Recall the question we asked earlier, why does this keep happening to me? We "learned during a fight" by understanding the individual does not want to make the necessary phone calls at all times of the day. They don't want to answer the phone calls at a certain time of the day. That cannot be the actions of an individual who wants to start a business. Does this mean that the person cannot earn a very substantial living? They may discover they have the qualities that make them a very marketable worker for any company. If this person is not willing to "Learn During The Fight," they will never open the door to "formulating the big picture" (ROUND 4) which is earning a good living. This process is particularly challenging because it involves evaluating and reevaluating situations all while fighting "LIFE."

ROUND 7
WHERE ARE WE IN THE FIGHT (RE-EVALUATION)

Learning during the fight requires reevaluation after the lessons are learned. Knowing where you are in a fight is essential to winning. In a boxing match, many different things during the fight have a dramatic impact on the direction of the contest. The impactful moments must be reevaluated. There is no set number of times a reevaluation can occur during a fight.

The fight against "LIFE" is no different. Many things happen to us that's extremely impactful to our mindset. Those things that happened to us during our fight with "LIFE" can be put in one word and that word is:

ADVERSITY

Dealing with adversity is a heavy factor in understanding how we build fortitude and mental strength. Let me emphasize the point:

NO ONE CAN GET THROUGH THE FIGHT AGAINST "LIFE" WITHOUT DEALING WITH ADVERSITY!

There is no way to predict when we will face that adversity. For some of us, we can go through many stages ("rounds") against "LIFE" and not have to deal with adversity. That path can lead to individuals believing that adversity will not come. Proceed with caution if you have this mindset because adversity will come. Let me emphasize this point:

A HUGE BENEFIT OF MENTAL CONDITIONING IS PREPARING OURSELVES TO DEAL WITH ADVERSITY!

No matter what stage ("round") we are currently experiencing in the fight against "LIFE," if we are not prepared to deal with adversity, we will certainly experience defeat. There are times in life when we honestly feel like we are winning. That certainly is a great feeling. When we are living in that moment, it's natural not to want to think about dealing with adversities or setbacks. To be clear, it is not being suggested that we constantly dwell on adversities and setbacks. Preparing and dwelling are two separate things. As we prepare, we put ourselves in a position to make the sharpest decisions under that adversity.

BOXING ANALOGY

MELDRICK TAYLOR VS. JULIO CESAR CHAVEZ I

The fight between Meldrick Taylor and Julio Cesar Chavez was a matchup between boxers of contrasting styles. Both fighters were highly proficient in their styles and confident in their ability. Both fighters were in their prime and the matchup was much anticipated. Chavez, already a legend, was undefeated in sixty-eight pro fights. Taylor was also undefeated in twenty-five fights. He was early in his career and attempting to build a legendary path. Taylor's hand and foot speed was second to none in the sport at that particular time. Chavez's style consisted of constant pressure using bruising punches and coming forward. His punches to the body made many opponents crumble.

As the fight began, Taylor's hand and foot speed proved too much for the more seasoned Chavez. Chavez could not seem to solve the problem of Taylor's speed. Clearly this was a sign of adversity in the ring for Chavez. Fighting through this challenge, Chavez continued his attack by constantly coming forward and throwing extremely hard punches that were landing. Chavez's punches were not landing with the volume and frequency as Taylor's were, but he landed with tremendous force. It was obvious that Taylor was winning the fight on points. However, the punches that Chavez landed caused tremendous damage to the body and face of Meldrick Taylor. Taylor's face was bleeding and he experienced very heavy swelling around the eyes, cheek bones and mouth. Blood was pouring out of the mouth of Taylor, indicating damage from the body shots had caused internal bleeding.

Both fighters were dealing with adversity. However, Taylor was winning the fight on points as they got ready to begin the 12th and final round. The fight was pitched in the final round, with both men throwing multiple punches and letting it all hang out. With about 17 seconds left in the fight, Chavez landed a crushing right-hand blow that sent Taylor crashing to the ground!

ADVERSITY

Taylor had never been down on the canvas before under these circumstances. If he gets up there's virtually no time for Chavez to throw anymore punches. Taylor does manage to get to his feet!! However, a fighter must respond to the referee to acknowledge that they are okay and ready to continue the fight. As he rose to his feet the referee stopped counting and asked Taylor if he was okay? Never having to deal with this type of adversity before, Taylor was mentally unprepared to prove to the referee that he was okay, even though he appeared to be. The referee asks Taylor "ARE YOU OKAY??" at which time Taylor did not respond and looked away. That response caused referee Richard Steele to stop the fight and award the victory to Chavez because he deemed Taylor unable to continue. That decision became one of the most controversial decisions by a referee in the history of boxing.

A fighter being knocked down is one of the biggest adversities they will face during their fighting career. Knowing what to do when you get up during this crisis it's not easy. Some fighters prepare for this moment. You see them get knocked down, get up, and start automatically doing what the referee wants to see. They will look the referee right in his eyes and respond immediately to his questions. You will occasionally see this even when a fighter is not physically there. Sometimes they cannot physically take steps, but you see them trying. That shows they trained for that adversity in the ring.

In the fight against "LIFE," we struggle with that question in preparing for adversity. If we prepare for adversity, are we preparing to lose? For that reason, many of us do not prepare mentally for it. In reality, however, there are numerous ways to prepare for adversity. This falls within the four principles of mental conditioning, specifically the principle of staying the course. Yes, we get knocked off the course in the fight against "LIFE," but it is all about how you get back on the course after your setback. We have to evaluate where we are in the fight after experiencing adversity. Meldrick Taylor got knocked down and when he got up, he needed to quickly assess where he was in the fight. There were two seconds left in the fight and he was ahead so the most important thing was to let the referee know he was ok. Had he achieved that, he probably would have won the fight.

LIFE ANALOGY

When a student is studying for an exam, it's imperative to know when they are understanding and retaining the information. It's a constant evaluation process. There are different approaches to knowing where you are when preparing for an exam. The thought of not passing the exam may never enter the mind of Student A. Conversely, Student B may be driven by the fear of not passing the examination. That fear may be the resounding discipline needed to study even when they do not want to do it. How they deal with their self-evaluation (Round 2) starts the cycle of dealing with adversity.

Neither student is wrong in their approach. Both students are right on course to maximize their ability to know where they are in the fight! This highlights and hits our Four Principles of Mental Conditioning. As a reminder:

1 – Self-Evaluation.

2 – Decision Making.

3 – Big Picture.

4 – Staying The Course.

√ In the case of the students studying for an exam, they must know their strong and weak areas. (Self-Evaluation Round 2)

√ The Student can make the determination to read specific areas more frequently than others based on that Self Evaluation (Decision Making Round 3)

√ How badly the student wants to pass the exam determines their study habits. (Big Picture Round 4)

√ There will be frustrating days of studying for several reasons. Can the student recover the next day and be effective in their studies? (Staying the Course)

This process is challenging because there are a tremendous number of emotions involved. Each Principle can invoke many emotions, resulting in us no longer caring about "where we are in the fight." Sometimes, it can be so overwhelming that we'll need help identifying "where we are in the fight" against "LIFE!"

ROUND 8
TRUST/INVEST IN YOUR TRAINERS

The process of conditioning our minds is a personal, private, and often lonely journey. Self-evaluation (Round 2) is the most essential principle in this process. The Principles outlined in the previous chapter and throughout this book also require our attention. However, the journey of Mental Conditioning requires help from other individuals. I like to call those individuals our "TRAINERS."

Before we go any further it is important to define the role of our "TRAINERS." In the fight against "LIFE" we are the ones who are in the ring. Nobody can fight for us. Nobody can absorb the punches from "LIFE" that we receive. However, when picked properly, our trainers can observe things that we sometimes do not see for ourselves. For those individuals to be effective, they are tasked with articulating what they see to us. This does not always mean we do exactly what our trainers say. This is where our trust/investment becomes very important.

Not just in boxing but in all sports, trainers and coaches are an important piece to the success of a fighter or team. Their role is important because they are the eyes on the outside seeing the situation directly looking in. In sports, the process of hiring a trainer or coach is extremely meticulous. Sometimes the process is lengthy. It requires careful analysis of their communication with the team/fighter. A trainer/coach can have great knowledge of the sport, but their ability and willingness to articulate what they see and know is a key ingredient. That chemistry is what makes the information relevant.

In our personal lives, the chemistry we develop is an overwhelming factor as to whether or not we can absorb the information the trainers of life are giving us. This process is an investment. Just like any other investment it takes time to come to fruition. Trust is a variable that needs to be developed. We must be able to trust what the trainer is telling us. This can be tricky. Earlier in this round I stated Mental Conditioning is a very private, personal, and at times, lonely journey. This still holds true, but we allow our "TRAINERS" to have a fine line of input in our fight against "LIFE." We must learn when to listen, what information to absorb versus discard, and to recognize when our vision is clouded. As our respect grows for the "TRAINERS" in our lives, we can and do allow their input to be more expansive and profound. But at the end of the day, we must remember that no matter how much respect we have for our trainers, they are not the one in the ring fighting our fight against "LIFE."

BRIEF BOXING ANALOGY

We referenced earlier in Round 6 (Learning During The Fight) the Muhammad Ali vs George Foreman fight. The point was made that Ali had a remarkably successful first round using his hand and foot speed to frustrate the bigger stronger Foreman. However, after the first round, Ali realized his movement and punch output were expending his energy more than the younger Foreman. Ali adjusted to stop moving as much. He resolved to lay on the ropes, allowing Foreman to throw unlimited hard punches at him. This strategy appeared to be suicide for Ali. After a successful first round in which his "TRAINERS" were very pleased, they were baffled at this tactic. So when he returns to the corner, the late, great and legendary trainer Angelo Dundee is livid. He tells Ali to get off the ropes! When the next round begins, Ali returns to the ropes again, allowing Foreman to throw devastating punches at him constantly. Now his trainer yells to Ali, "GET OFF THE ROPES!" Nobody had ever absorbed this kind of punishment from the young champion. Round after round, Ali would return to his corner and hear the same thing from Dundee. As the fight continued, Ali would respond to Dundee, "Shut up, I know what I'm doing." The respect Ali had for his trainer was extremely high, however he fully understood that he was the one who was in the ring and knew what his body could take. Ali won the fight by wearing Foreman out from throwing all those punches. What he saw in the ring worked and he stood firm to what he believed.

So, the line is very thin about when we should and shouldn't follow what our "Trainers" are telling us. That said, the impact of "Trainers" in our lives can sometimes be profound. Sometimes, that input is not particularly overwhelming. Not always do the big words of wisdom ring most effectively in our mindset. Sometimes, they point out what we already know but are not observing now. Our willingness to hear the advice boils down to the trust we build in our trainers.

BOXING ANALOGY
SUGAR RAY LEONARD VS. TOMMY HEARNS I

*A trainer's influence was evident during the first fight between Sugar Ray Leonard and Tommy Hearns. This was certainly one of the biggest fights that could be made in boxing at that particular time. Two young strong undefeated fighters in their absolute primes fighting each other. It almost feels like the pressure is too much and too much is on the line when the best of the best face off against each other in the ring. On one side of the ring you had Ray Leonard who was next in line to become the face of boxing, primed to take the position from the now retired Muhammed Ali. In the other corner you have Thomas "THE HITMAN" Hearns, an undefeated knockout artist coming out of the infamous Kronk Gym in Detroit led by the late, great trainer Emmanuel Steward. The matchup was competitive with the edge going to Leonard early. From the outset Leonard's skill level, speed and rugged determination appeared to be the difference in the fight. However, as the middle rounds of the fight approached, Hearns's surprising ability to outbox Leonard started to establish a clear dominance that diminished the early lead Leonard had built. In fact, Hearns had now started to establish a lead of his own in the fight. As the fight started to slip away from Leonard his "TRAINER" played a critical role in the outcome. Between rounds **twelve** and **thirteen** his trainer offered the most inspiring advice of the night. As Dundee wipes his fighter down, he tells him, "YOU ARE BLOWING IT NOW SON! YOU ARE BLOWING IT!" Those infamous words inspired Leonard to turn it on in the next rounds. Over the next two rounds, Leonard pressured Hearns and ultimately scored a technical knockout just a round and half later. He would later say the words of advice from his trainer proved to be an impactful factor of the final result of the fight. This is a really good example. So many variables come into play regarding "TRUSTING/INVESTING IN OUR TRAINERS." Here is Leonard, battling hard for twelve rounds and starting to lose the battle and having to hear from his trainer "YOU ARE BLOWING IT NOW SON, YOU ARE BLOWING IT." That could have discouraged or even angered him, forcing his mindset to change. He could have stopped trying out of frustration, just finished the fight, and let the judges decide. He took a different path and decided to step up his attack and press hard to hurt Hearns. What factor made him use the advice from his corner as a positive?*

TRUST!

Any advice given to us is only as good as our trust in the person offering it to us. Often the best information given to us by our trusted trainers is not necessarily specific in advising direction. It can be an observation pointing out something we may suspect already. While Dundee does provide plenty of technical boxing advice, it was more of a general observation that provided the most pivotal information for Leonard's victory. Naturally, Leonard probably felt the fight turning in Hearns's favor. However, Dundee made the point aloud and delivered just the direction Leonard needed. Most importantly, Leonard trusted the advice to be true and accurate.

We have used the word trust multiple times in this round. Why is it so important? Our trainers can and will give us information/advice that will sometimes be difficult to hear. It is very possible our minds naturally will become defensive. Some of those natural defensive mental tactics are to claim excuses as to why information/advice is not valid or accurate. Some of those excuses include accusing the trainer of:

1 – Being Incompetent.

2 – Being Jealous.

3 – Being Envious.

4 – Not having your best interest at heart.

As we build trust in our trainers, the previous excuses listed are clearly out of the question. The opponent, "LIFE," will test that relationship.

LIFE ANALOGY

Relationships challenge our decision-making skills (Round 3). Emotions are an intricate part of relationships; sometimes, it is hard to see or admit what is happening. A trusted "trainer" can play a significant role here. That "Trainer" is on the outside looking in, so they can point out what they see.

At some point in our lives, we have cause to deal with toxic behavior or find ourselves in a toxic relationship. Sometimes we develop a pattern of going into one toxic relationship after another. The pattern may not be obvious to the person involved, or it could be something the individual may not be ready or willing to admit to themselves. A trusted "Trainer" can point it out and effectively impact a person's direction. Simply pointing out the fact that there is a pattern of toxic relationships is effective, sound advice. We need trusted "Trainers" for guidance when emotions or stakes are high. Sometimes we need them to point out the obvious, like Dundee saying, "YOU ARE BLOWING IT SON, YOU ARE BLOWING IT!" Other times, we need them to give us specific instructions on how to move forward and how we should. And sometimes, we may need our "Trainers" to simply listen. All of those roles hold equal significance.

The relationship between a trusted "Trainer" and an individual involves complex reasoning. While our trusted "Trainer" can provide potential for meaningful direction, we must remember that our mindset is paramount.

A prerequisite for being a trusted "Trainer" is for that person to know your tendencies. They should know your strengths and weaknesses if possible. While they offer everything previously mentioned, it's really up to us to understand what we can or cannot implement. As important as their input is, there will be situations in which we will have to forgo their advice/ guidance. It does not mean that trust is not there. It is more of a reflection of strong "self-evaluation" (Round 2), which is essential to building mental strength. We did not talk specifically about who our "Trainer" might be. Mainly because that person can be anyone. The most important thing is for the person to meet the criteria stated during this round. As such, your "Trainer" can be a family member, spouse, parent, friend, pastor, psychotherapist, mindset coach or even a casual friend in some cases. It's not necessarily the person who is closest to you. In boxing it is not uncommon to have fathers introduce their sons to the sport and train them. It is equally common that the father being his son's trainer ultimately does not work out. The trainer position in our lives holds great value and is tested with every life challenge. So the criteria of choosing our "Trainers" requires constant evaluation. An effective trainer may be great for a season; you must make the necessary change after some time. Add this to the long list of reasons why self-evaluation is important to our everyday progress and growth!

ROUND 9
KNOCKDOWN

Sometimes, even with the best, most trusted "Trainers" (Round 8), the best "Self- Evaluation" (Round 2) and a clear "Big Picture" (Round 4), we can still suffer a "KNOCKDOWN" in our fight against "Life." Without exception, we all have suffered knockdowns at some point in our lives. Some examples of what a "KNOCKDOWN" in life can look like are below:

√ Disappointment
√ Loss Of Loved Ones
√ Loss Of Employment
√ Loss of Marriage
√ Loss Of Relationships
√ Not Being what you want when you want it
√ Coming Up Short on Goals
√ Financial Setbacks
√ Loss of Self

Be careful of the wording. "KNOCKDOWN" is not a Knockout!! There is a very distinct difference. No matter how many times a person gets **knocked down**, they can always get up. When a person gets Knocked Out, there is no getting up. I am reminded of once hearing boxer Evander Holyfield talk about a fighter enduring pain during a fight. He stated:

"AS LONG AS YOU CAN FEEL THE PAIN, YOU IN THE FIGHT! WHEN YOU CAN'T FEEL THE PAIN, YOU OUT!"

I always thought that was a great analogy. As we endure the

challenges of life, we experience so much pain. In many instances, we try to run from that pain. We do that in so many different ways. Sometimes we abuse our bodies physically. In other situations, we abuse our mindset. We abuse our mindset by no longer performing our four principles.

Self-Evaluation	Decision Making
Big Picture	Staying The Course

The thought of being knocked down is not something any of us looks forward to. Look at how powerful the process of training our mind in the fight against "LIFE" is. We train to identify pain when we get knocked down. "AS LONG AS YOU FEEL THE PAIN, YOU STILL IN THE FIGHT." The pain you feel identifies you want to get better. It shows you want to get back up and "stay the course." When you don't feel anything, it means you do not care. Having a full understanding of this requires us to get out of the normal rhythm of thinking and basic instinct. Nobody wants to be knocked down or hurt in our lives, yet here we are, welcoming the pain. It requires mental training to embrace that pain as an identifier of your ability to stay in the fight against "LIFE." Big Picture (Round 4) is one of the four principles of mental conditioning. It allows us to keep driving forward even when we get knocked down. This is a precise example of why the big picture (Round 4) is important.

If we do not properly identify our big picture (Round 4) or fail to have one, there will be no pain upon getting knocked down. There will be no pain because as an individual we no longer care. So there's nothing to be disappointed about. No purpose translates into just not caring. When there is no **life destination** to drive to, there are no feelings about where we are in the fight against "LIFE." So, when "LIFE" hits us hard and we go down, why bother to get up? One would think if there is no pain, you can easily get up. That may be physically true, however mentally there is no desire to get up and move forward. The pain comes from the emotion of being knocked off course. When you can feel that pain you are motivated to get up and show you can get back on course. Sometimes, the thought of not reaching your goal is the pain that makes you get up. When we watch a boxing match up and a fighter gets knocked down, what do you think makes them get up?

BOXING ANALOGY
José Louis Castillo vs. Diego Corrales

The battle between these two warriors epitomizes all we can see during a boxing match that parallels life. Again, in this particular match, you have two young fighters of remarkably high skill level who were in their prime. The fight proved competitive going back and forth with both men having their share of the upper hand. Late in the fight Castillo seemed to be able to establish his dominance over Corrales. The punches seem to be taking a toll on Corrales and his face began to show the effects of the punishment. He had heavy swelling of the face, and his eye was swollen shut. Castillo landed punch after punch and finally badly hurt Corrales sending him to the canvas numerous times. The pain in his face was apparent. However, he got up each time after the knockdowns, which was incredible. As you watch you can't help but to wonder, "HOW?" How is this man rising to his feet after being "Knocked Down" and clearly hurting very badly. In the 10th round of the fight, we got an answer. The physical pain he was feeling was nothing compared to the pain he was feeling at the thought of losing the fight. Had he lost the desire to win the fight there would be no more pain. That would mean he would not have gotten up.

In the 10th round, Corrales continued to throw hard shots even though he was battered and bloodied. His punches were also connecting and severely hurt Castillo. Castillo, exhausted from giving out and receiving punishment was out on his feet as Corrales continued to wail away on him. The referee had no other recourse but to stop the fight and save Castillo from further punishment. For Corrales to win this fight was an unbelievable turn of events to witness. It proved to be an uncanny example of overcoming a "Knockdown." As a side note to Diego Corrales's passion to win, I am reminded of the image of him losing to Floyd Mayweather and conducting an interview after. In that fight Corrales was absorbed a great deal of punishment from Mayweather. He did get knocked down numerous times on that night as well. Just as in the Castillo fight, he would not stay down. However, the difference on this night was his trainer stepped in and stopped the fight. I remember literal tears falling down Corrales' face as the fight ended. This was a clear example that the pain of losing the fight outweighed the physical pain he was absorbing, which once again highlights the point, "As long as you can feel the pain, you still in the game."

We must consciously build mental muscle that enables us to understand we can and Do get "Knocked Down." When we get knocked down, do we know for sure what is going to happen? We do not know how we are going to react. We know neither of these things, and we don't know what level of pain we will feel or not. Mental preparation gives us an advantage to deal with Knockdowns.

Earlier in the Round we talked about the "Big Picture" being a great exercise to build Mental Muscle for life's "Knockdown." "Self-evaluation" is probably the primary exercise needed to build Mental Muscle to deal with life's "Knockdowns." "Self-Evaluation" (Round 2) is always specifically driven to each individual. However, this is a rare occurrence where we must have a common piece of self-evaluation. If we believe we cannot be Knocked Down, when it inevitably happens, we have no way of knowing what to do next. Now, getting back up and back on the course becomes more complex and complicated because you were completely shocked that you even got "Knocked Down."

CRITICAL POINT

> KNOCKDOWNS AND KNOCKOUTS
> ARE TWO DIFFERENT THINGS!

We all get knocked down but many of us can get up and back on course. A critical variable of being able to get up is first accepting that you could be knocked down.

TWO QUICK BOXING ANALOGIES TO END ROUND 9

1 – Ali vs Foreman (Discussed Previously)

In the 8th Round, Ali landed a smashing combination to George Foreman's head sending the exhausted champion down to the canvas. The image is embedded in my head of seeing him lying on his back with his head raised off the canvas looking up, exhausted. Although his eyes appeared clear, he did not attempt to get up. Foreman would later say he was shocked that he was actually "Knocked Down!" Therefore, rendering him to make no attempt to get up.

2 – Andre Ward vs Sergey Kovalev

Another highly anticipated matchup between two of the top fighters in their division. Andre Ward was considered a smart, skillful boxer. Sergey Kovalev was considered one of the hardest hitting punchers in boxing. In preparing for the fight, Ward's "Trainer" (Round 8) the great Virgil Hunter, advised him that to win there was a good chance he was going to get "Knock Down." In the second round of the fight, Kovalev hit Ward with a hard right hand and knocked him down. Ward did get up, recovered, and went on to win the fight. He later stated his "Trainer" who had prepared him to be "Knocked Down" was critical to him being able to withstand the adversity of that situation, ultimately getting him the win in one of the biggest challenges of his career!

ROUND 10
GET UP, GRAB AND HOLD

So, you got knocked down. What's next?? First thing's first - you have to Get Up! Being able to get back up in life is not always a basic instinct. When a baby starts learning how to walk, that journey will have many knockdowns. They struggle with their balance. They learn how to fall without getting badly hurt. They learn how to brace themselves from being more seriously injured. They may use their hands to protect themselves from hitting their heads or other body parts. Eventually, their confidence starts to grow, and they take more chances which means more risks. As parents, the first thing we teach our children regarding falling is to "Get Up!" Sometimes they fall pretty hard, yet we tell them immediately, "Get Up!" So, we are taught to get up after falling from an early age. That is a lesson we never stray away from no matter how old we get.

As we advance in life, so does recovery from a Knockdown. After we get up, there is an element of pain we have to deal with. This is where we adapt the strategy of Grab-and-Hold. In the fight against "LIFE," after a knockdown (Round 9), we are still reeling from the effects. Just because we got up does not mean we are recovered. There are things we must do to steady ourselves and prevent us from going down again.

CRITICAL POINT

MULTIPLE KNOCKDOWNS FROM THE SAME SITUATION CAUSES HIGH RISK OF BEING "KNOCKED OUT!" Sometimes steadying before attempting to get up is a huge part of preventing additional knock-downs or a possible knockout.

BOXING ANALOGY
ZAB JUDAH VS. KOSTYA TSZYU

Yet again, another highly anticipated matchup between two highly talented fighters. On one side of the ring was Kostya Tszyu, a veteran of the ring who was still in his prime. He was a Power Puncher with experience of knocking his opponents and putting them on the ground. On the other side of the ring is Zab Judah, a young fighter with limitless potential and tremendous natural ability. Judah had extremely fast hands, was quick on his feet and had good punching power. Judah is the younger, least experienced fighter of the two. Tszyu had been in a high-profile fight before, while this was the biggest stage Judah had been on for a fight. Without question, Judah was the future of boxing at that particular time.

As the fight started, the exuberance and youth of Judah was apparent. His punches were quick and pronounced. He landed some very hard punches to Tszyu's head early in the fight. The speed of Judah seemed to give Tszyu trouble in the first round. However, in the second round Tszyu was able to settle the fight's pace down. He was methodically landing more power shots and settling the fight down. At the end of the second round Tsyzu landed a hard right hand directly to Judah's chin, sending him crashing to the canvas. Judah immediately tried to get up as soon as he hit the canvas. He was on the ground for a second. He absorbed a hard punch. Judah would have been best served to steady himself before attempting to "GET UP." As he began to rise to his feet it was obvious that his eyes were completely glazed and not focused at all. As he got to his feet his legs were completely unsteady. He struggled to try to stay up but to no avail. His legs collapsed as he rose to his feet, and he stumbled to the canvas again. Upon going down the second time, the referee stopped the fight resulting in Judah losing the fight. As soon as the Referee Jay Nady stopped the fight, Judah's eyes cleared, his legs were steady, and he appeared ready to continue! Those precious seconds trying to steady himself would have meant all the difference in the world. There is no guarantee he would have won the fight, but it appears he would have been able to continue to do the good work he was doing until the knockdown.

In our relationships we certainly experience heartache. Rejection is truly a knockdown. Sometimes, the response is to stay down before we start another relationship. The period of staying down can afford us the time to do our self-evaluation (Round 2) of where we are. Are we too emotionally fragile to begin another relationship? Through our self-evaluation, we can take that time to see when we feel steady enough to get up. In our Boxing analogy, had Judah taken the time to evaluate himself, he likely would have gotten up on more steady legs to continue. This is where strong Mental Conditioning comes into play. When down, our natural instinct is to get up right away. That is understandable. We have to train to fight against that natural instinct. The round was coming to an end, so it was likely all he had to do was stand up and he could make it out of the round. We cannot promise any results of the fight, but he would have at least been able to continue.

There are times in our fight against "LIFE" in which we can rise to our feet and stand on steady legs, but that does not necessarily mean we can continue as normal. Here is when we have to "GRAB AND HOLD." "LIFE" is always evolving and progressing. There will be situations where there is not enough time to get completely steady before you get up. We may be able to stay down long enough to ensure we can stand up on steady legs, but now what? Our legs may be steady enough to stand up, but our minds may be heavily clouded, making the decision-making difficult. What does grab and hold look like in our everyday lives?

BOXING ANALOGY

Evander Holyfield vs. Riddick Bowe
Round 10

Evander Holyfield fought Riddick Bowe in an epic battle. The two fighters ended up fighting each other in multiple bouts. The first fight featured Holyfield as the champion and Bowe as the up-and-coming challenger. This was a very hard-fought battle throughout. Bowe appeared to have the edge. The tenth round of the fight proved to be one of the most exciting rounds in heavyweight history. Going into the round, Holyfield appeared tired, and the younger Bowe looked fresher and in control. In the opening seconds of the round Bowe hit Holyfield with a crushing uppercut that literally put Holyfield out on his feet. Although he was on his feet, he was badly hurt with plenty of time left in the round. How could he make it through the round without being "KNOCKED OUT?" Answer: "GRAB AND HOLD!" Holyfield was stumbling around the ring. Each time Bowe got close Holyfield would "Grab and Hold." Even though Bowe was still trying to throw punches at him, Holyfield would "Grab and Hold" on for dear life. Now technically excessive "Grabbing and Holding" is illegal in the rules of a boxing match. However sometimes a fighter has to do what is necessary to weather the storm and clear their head. In this case, Holyfield continued to "Grab and Hold" for another minute or so of the round. Eventually his head began to clear, and his legs were steady, and Holyfield began an offensive assault on Bowe who was now tiring due to his high output of punches. Holyfield badly hurt Bowe with a barrage of punches as the tenth round ended. The key to his offensive attack was getting himself composed by "Grabbing and Holding" after being out on his feet.

Our life situations often call for some tactical mindset strategies. Occurrences require us to recover before we can move forward with a clear head to make sound decisions. Grab and hold can physically look like many different things in our everyday lives. It largely depends on the situation we are facing. One thing that will be constant in this process is using the principles of mental conditioning:

1 – Self-Evaluation – First admit that you have been "KNOCKED DOWN" or even out on your feet.

2—Decision Making—When our heads are not clear due to absorbing a heavy blow from "LIFE," our decision-making is not sharp. It can be quite clouded.

3 – Big Picture – When our mind is unclear and we are hurt, we need to evaluate the importance of that BIG PICTURE. Do I want this, or am I going to quit?

4 – Staying The Course – "KNOCKDOWNS" takes us off the course. Are you willing to get back on course!!! Is that "BIG PICTURE" worth it?

The principles are a guide to what grab and hold looks like in real-life situations and how to utilize it. Sometimes, in the fight against "LIFE," grab and hold plays out in the form of not making any decisions at all. Sometimes, our emotions are so high that making a sound decision is impossible. Grab and hold is critical because we cannot stop fighting (LIVING LIFE). It is possible to delay decisions until your mind becomes clear.

We constantly discuss the critical importance of self-evaluations (Round 2) in building Mental Muscle. So here is a little curveball. This small window of grab and hold is the short period in which self-evaluation is not recommended. Yes, we must evaluate ourselves to admit we are hurt. However, our state of mind when we are badly hurt is temporary. In-depth self-evaluation during this time can damage our ability to move forward to get past the knockdown. In these situations, the more prudent strategy is focusing more intently on regaining our steady mindset and evaluating what that looks like.

ROUND 11

GET BACK UP AND STAY THE COURSE

Okay! You got up and had to briefly grab and hold (Round 10). Now what? As you are taking these steps, your head will begin to clear, and the process of self-evaluation (Round 2) can once again begin. Starting this process can be a bit tricky, as time is a major factor.

We can take as much time as necessary to hold and recover in certain situations. Unfortunately, we will often not have the luxury of unlimited time to recover from a knockdown. Regardless of either situation, the process of getting back on course must begin. This is one of the critical moments in the fight against "LIFE" that is very challenging. We always hear the saying that "life is not easy." We would all agree, but defining what that entails is important. The challenge of trying to get back and stay on course in our lives, sometimes in the face of permanent scarring, can seem impossible. This is exactly what leads to us giving up on life. To be clear, us giving up on life is not always taking our own life by suicide. Many of us are breathing and extremely healthy with no intentions of taking their own life but still have given up on life.

We are all born with a sense of direction of where we want to go in life. Without definition however, that direction cannot be validated. So, let's define what direction looks like. We talked in the previous round about an infant learning how to walk. That is an infant's process of the mind having direction. Babies imitate the things they see their parents do. That is already subconsciously a defining direction. I can recall seeing video clips of infants trying to mimic things they have obviously seen their parents or someone else do. One video showed a young child who was not even walking yet attempting to put a straw inside the small hole of a coffee cup. After about four or five very good attempts, she threw the cup and straw out of complete frustration. In another video, a young baby capable of walking but not yet verbal, was attempting to put his sock on. After several attempts, he stood up and threw the sock across the room, spinning his whole body because he threw it so hard. Both videos were frankly comical to watch, but it shows great development in our sense of marching towards our goals while enduring challenges to stay the course.

Why did those babies get so frustrated? They saw something somebody else was doing and they wanted to be able to do it for themselves. While it may seem trivial, it establishes a sense of direction that we all have experienced at some point in our lives. The babies fell off the course because one could not put the straw in the cup and the other could not put the sock on. Throwing the objects was the equivalent of a knockdown. I can assure you after a short break, if you give those two babies the items back, they will try again. That is their attempt to get back on course. These examples are much simpler than situations we deal with as adults. We have much more baggage that fits into our equations, which makes it one thousand times more difficult to get back and stay on course.

As adults, we experience setbacks in which we never really correct. So, we learn that it is not the end of the world to have a setback. Knowing there are no guarantees makes staying the course difficult. When a fighter gets hit, goes down, gets up and then grabs a hold, there is no guarantee of victory. It is certainly a real possibility that the fighter can go down numerous times after getting up. With those odds however, what would make a fighter stay the course? Big picture plays a paramount role here along with the four principals. Of course, our self-evaluation identifies our big picture, which is the prize. This begs the question:

"IS THE PRIZE WORTH THE PAIN?"

You will get the answer to this question when you identify if you can stay the course. The pain can be overwhelming. In relationships, we put large amounts of emotion, time, energy, and sacrifice into our circles of influence. At some point, we evaluate those relationships as to where they stand in our big picture of life. No relationship under any circumstance is perfect. We certainly all go through ups and downs. It seems the downs put us in more of a position to be forced to make decisions regarding the relationship. Getting knocked down in a relationship places you firmly at a crossroad. Do you want to get up and stay the course? There is no right or wrong answer. Some people evaluate their marriage as being an untouchable big picture. Even with that determination, there still will have to be a constant evaluation.

"LIFE" never stops its enduring pursuit, and relationships are no different. Due to varying circumstances, a decision may have to be made within a short time, meaning an individual may still be reeling from pain inflicted by their partner while simultaneously being asked to decide immediately whether or not they wish to stay the course of their marriage. Imagine that!

If your big picture is clearly determined, it potentially makes the decision much clearer, but clarity is not a pathway to ease. The decision will still be difficult. However, establishing our big picture allows us to do things **mentally** we never thought we would be able to do otherwise. The power of the mind is extraordinary if we understand how to train it.

It can also be an identifier of when is when. We cannot discuss staying the course without addressing that sometimes the relationship has run its course and come to its inevitable end. Many will consider it to be negative, however it can essentially be positive. The critical determining factor is honest self-evaluation and commitment to the four principles of mental conditioning. There will be situations in which it is in our best interest to move forward and abandon a particular course. It sounds like a defeat to even write that. However, when the decision is made properly using the four principles of mental conditioning, it can lead to victory in the overall fight against "LIFE."

BOXING ANALOGY
GERALD MCCLELLAN VS. NIGEL BENN

This will become one of the more brutal fights in the ring. Two exceptionally good fighters and warriors matching up in their prime. At the time Gerald McClellan was one of the clear rising stars of the sport. Nigel Benn was not a famous fighter in the United States but was one of the stars of British boxing in the United Kingdom. McClellan was another member out of the famed Kronk gym run by the legendary Emanuel Steward. He started the first round with supreme confidence, even though he had traveled out of the United States to fight on the home turf of Nigel Benn in the UK. McClellan came out firing bombs and Benn was standing there ready to exchange. He landed numerous hard shots to the head of Benn, hurting him badly and knocking him out of the ring! Benn somehow managed to get up and return to the ring before the count of ten. While being badly hurt it was apparent that Benn's "BIG PICTURE" was not to lose on his home turf to an outsider. He used survival tactics of "GRAB AND HOLD AND MOVE" until his head began to clear. Eventually his head cleared. Benn was able to get back "ON COURSE" by staying aggressive and fighting his rugged fight and grinding it out.

The fight went back and forth throughout the next nine rounds with both guys landing damaging punches. At various occurrences both guys appeared to be staggered and hurt. Both fighters could recover and fight on "STAYING THE COURSE" to their ultimate "BIG PICTURE" which was victory! In the tenth round Benn landed some good shots to McClellan's head, but nothing he had not absorbed already in the previous rounds. Something was different this time because he backed away and kneeled to one knee. Usually when we see a boxer take a knee, he knows he is buzzed and maybe needs a quick second to steady himself. After gathering themselves fighters commonly will get up easily at around 8 seconds. This situation was slightly unusual at the start because McClellan had taken some shots, but he did not appear to be terribly affected. Nevertheless, he fell to one knee and took the referee's count.

"One! Two! Three! Four!"

The whole building, including his team and everybody watching on television, fully expected McClellan to rise to his feet by the count of eight. However, to the surprise of everyone watching, the referee reached the count of "TEN" and he did not rise. The fight was over.

Amazingly, just after the referee reached the count of ten, McClellan immediately rose to his feet indicating his head was clear and he knew what was happening. When he was on his knee *awaiting the count of ten, McClellan blinked his eyes badly. As he rose to his feet after the ten count, he blinked his eyes badly as he walked back to his corner. Within minutes he collapsed in his corner, fell unconscious, and was ultimately carried out on a stretcher and rushed to the hospital. They performed emergency brain surgery. McClellan suffered permanent effects including blindness, loss of ability to walk, loss of short-term memory, and difficulties hearing.*

Looking at the analogy, both went into the ring on course to attempt to achieve victory. The desire to win burned in both fighters. It was evident by the brutality and punishment both fighters took in the ring. When Benn was knocked out of the ring in the first round, he had to decide to "Stay the Course," in his case, he did. In that tenth round McClellan was forced to make the same decision when he took the knee. He ultimately decided it was time to abandon that course.

Let's look at how powerful this is. Something he felt physically in his "Self-Evaluation" allowed him to make a "Clear Decision." I am quite sure that decision was not easy but something he physically felt made it a "Clear Decision." At that moment we can only speculate that he felt something that he believed was seriously wrong that could endanger his life. That decision could have very well saved his life. Maybe if he had gotten up off the knee and continued to fight, he would have gotten hit again and suffered fatal damage. Honest "Self-Evaluation" of his physical condition changed his "Big Picture" in seconds. It shifted from winning a fight to just wanting to live.

We are faced with similar decisions in our everyday lives. It takes many hours of training in your Mental Conditioning Gym to put your mindset in positions to be clear about whether or not to stay the course. The reward of training our mind properly is endless regarding where life's journeys can go. There is an enormous amount of trust that must go into that training to make decisions that are positive and life changing. As we experience life changing decisions based on our mental conditioning, it is important to equally embrace the results of the hard work.

ROUND 12

THE THRILL OF VICTORY AND AGONY OF DEFEAT

Going through the work required to get through twelve rounds of Mental Conditioning is objectively difficult. Implementing the Four Principles throughout the fight against "LIFE" is particularly challenging. Each round you win is one step closer to your goal, which is to reach your life's destination. Even when you lose a round or get "KNOCKED DOWN," getting up is a huge step toward winning the fight. Once we reach our life's destination after a hard-fought fight, you have achieved either "THE THRILL OF VICTORY" or "THE AGONY OF DEFEAT." The feeling of accomplishment that comes along with "THE THRILL OF VICTORY" is not easy to articulate in words. "THE AGONY OF DEFEAT" is equally challenging to convey. What do they both mean to and for our mindset? A great deal of training must take place to accept "THE THRILL OF VICTORY OR AGONY OF DEFEAT." Sometimes, the journey is so treacherous that it is unbelievable that it is over - no matter the result!

Accepting the final result is as important as any part of the previous rounds discussed. As much progress was made to get to this point, it would have been all for nothing if we could not accept the thrill of victory. Forward progress is made when we learn how to strengthen our mind to accept the final result. In round six, we talked about learning during the round, but there are also essential lessons to be learned in victory! The jubilation of success brings confidence to go forward after victory is won.

BOXING ANALOGY

Evander Holyfield Beats Mike Tyson in Their First Fight

For this example, we must clearly understand what went on before and after the fight as opposed to the actual fight. Going into the first fight with Mike Tyson, Evander Holyfield had been on a downward slide in his career. He had lost the title only to regain it and lose it again in a horrific performance against Michael Moorer. After the fight with Moorer, Holyfield was diagnosed with a heart condition that would cause him to retire. He would eventually return to Boxing, but with a couple subpar performances, including an unimpressive victory over Bobby Czyz, who was lightly regarded at that time, and a knockout loss to Riddick Bowe in their third fight.

Holyfield then signed to fight Tyson. Many people believed that he was washed up. He certainly was not fighting with the same confidence, precision, and sharpness we had seen from Holyfield throughout his career. He later stated during his training camp for the fight with Tyson, "My sparring partners were whipping me up." So Holyfield was preparing to fight Tyson (who was a champion and still regarded as a top heavyweight in the world) while he could not last more than 2 or 3 rounds with his sparring partners! Although Holyfield was a supremely confident fighter, he certainly had to have experienced some loss of confidence.

As fight night drew near, nobody believed Holyfield would win at this point in his career. Yet to the surprise of everyone, he won and looked fantastic doing it! What followed was truly beautiful to witness. I recall in Holyfield's post-fight interviews that an air of confidence could only be attributed to accepting "THE THRILL OF VICTORY." Holyfield was susceptible to up-and-down performances and physical decline due to his age at this point in his career. However, this was the greatest, most satisfying victory of his career. Most notably, he had a rematch with Tyson and fought Michael Moorer again (whom he had previously lost his titles to), achieving victories in both fights. He had a renewed sense of confidence evident in how he fought.

In sports, we see the mindset change when an athlete or team accepts the "THRILL OF VICTORY." When you see a team win a championship, and that team stays together, they play like champions. In professional basketball, we have seen teams build dynasties over the past three decades and win multiple championships even as the talent declines due to age. The championship mentality of accepting the "THRILL OF VICTORY" is a mindset of progressive thinking.

BOXING ANALOGY
Andre Ward vs. Sergey Kovalev (2)

Sometimes accepting victory brings peace and satisfaction in life. Andre Ward versus Sergey Kovalev was a fitting example. The two warriors had two epic battles. In the second battle, Andre Ward prevailed for the second time. Both fights proved to be competitive battles. There was adversity for Andre Ward throughout both fights. He knew this would be a challenging opponent. Andre Ward had experienced a very gratifying career up to this point. He had achieved many goals that he had set out to obtain in the sport. This would be his crowning achievement. He had won the middleweight tournament that had never been seen in boxing. He had amassed numerous championships. This fight would be one of his last challenges.

Kovalev was a devastating puncher and was a tremendous threat to Andre Ward's undefeated record. The first fight was a close battle in which Andre Ward won by decision. The rematch was a chance to prove who truly was the best fighter. Ward was unsure after the first fight if he would take the rematch. After much thought, he decided this would be his last fight unbeknownst to anyone. The fight was tough for Ward as he dealt with many different things we discussed in the previous rounds. His knee injury caused him to consider canceling the fight at the last minute. He decided to go forward, and fight as scheduled. He dealt with adversity during the fight by dealing with that painful knee. He put it behind him and continued to fight. He then began attacking the body of Kovalev, damaging him to the point of the referee having to stop the fight. As Andre Ward won the fight, he victoriously raised his hand, truly accepting the victory. It was not just the victory of the night but the victory of his career. Andre Ward subsequently retired after this fight. Although he was still in the prime of his career. Age-wise he had years to continue to fight at a very high level and achieve tremendous monetary gain. However, he decided to step away from the sport and has not returned. Ward talks about the battle of staying out of the ring and staying retired. Some days he is happy that he stepped away and has not returned. Some days he does have the urge to continue to fight. Ultimately accepting the victory of his career is truly what put him at peace. As he sits back and contemplates those moments of wanting to return to the ring, the reality of accepting the victory for his career allows him to be at peace with his decision.

Our lives must reflect the same progressive thinking. It is important to train our minds to accept the wins in our lives. At times it may not be the ultimate win we are looking for but accepting the thrill of victory clears and prepares your mind to move forward. We may hear or catch ourselves saying things like, "Yea, that was a win, but…" It is important to recognize that win is productive forward progress. This is an essential part of building Mental Muscle to display confidence in the result of all the work we put in. Our decision making is now based on something we already have found the answer to. This allows us to build greater wins soon. We strive in the fight against "LIFE" to raise our hand in the thrill of victory.

A part of the journey in the fight against "LIFE" is the "AGONY OF DEFEAT." This obviously is a painful part of the journey. As we go through the twelve rounds, we will learn the "Agony Of Defeat" is just as important and in some cases, it can prove to be the most effective tool in reaching our big picture in life. We spend the time in the Mental Conditioning Gym to prepare, we spend time putting in the work throughout the twelve rounds to execute as effectively as possible. The unfortunate reality is sometimes it is not good enough for the victory. However, even in "THE AGONY OF DEFEAT," we learn valuable lessons. The lessons include how to prepare better, how much we can endure, and proves we can get back on the course after being knocked off. The natural thinking behind "The Agony of Defeat" is to believe all the work put in was for nothing but it is the exact opposite (provided we did put in the necessary work). Our minds will be ready to receive the information even when experiencing the agony of defeat. Using the Four Principles of Mental Conditioning provides the blueprint to learn from the agony of defeat.

SELF EVALUATION – It is extremely difficult to assess what happened when dealing with "The Agony Of Defeat" but it is critical for the comeback. The Previous 11 rounds prepared us for this. We will identify why the results ended up the way they were. Sometimes "The Thrill Of Victory" does not allow us to make that assessment. When we train our minds to perform Self-Evaluations" after the agony of defeat, we learn it will probably be one of the most meticulous evaluations we can execute. It brings a calming peace to the agony of defeat. We often hear people say: the worst thing that happened to them turned out to be the best thing that happened to them.

DECISION MAKING – After experiencing the agony of defeat, we can have heightened decision-making skills. It makes us replay each moment repeatedly in our heads. We fall into the habit of questioning every decision made that led up to being defeated. We must train our minds to accept this to achieve our eventual success in the scope of our big picture. Sometimes that means a rematch of the circumstances against the opponent "LIFE." Accepting the agony of defeat and analyzing what happened and the decisions made will prevent us from making the same ineffective decisions.

BIG PICTURE—"The agony of defeat" is a tremendous tool for reinforcing our big picture. After experiencing defeat, the reasonable question is, "Do I really want this?" Is this truly my big picture? This evidence again shows that the agony of defeat can be a great tool for true Self-evaluation.

STAYING THE COURSE – This goes hand in hand with our big picture. What does it look like when we reinforce our big picture after experiencing the agony of defeat? Staying the course is exactly what it looks like. It is challenging to keep trying when things do not go our way. In most situations it is not necessarily physically challenging. To mentally reset ourselves, you must resolve to get back in line and challenge "LIFE" again. This takes clear and precise direction and mental strength.

One Final Boxing Analogy

BOXING ANALOGY
ERROL SPENCE VS. TERENCE CRAWFORD

At the time of publication, this fight recently happened. This clash has embodied many parallels between life and Mental Conditioning. The Boxing community had long anticipated the fight between Errol Spence and Terence Crawford. The anticipation of the fight was legendary. We once again have two undefeated fighters with all of the championship titles on the line battling each other. The opinions of the fight split 50-50 on who would be the winner. As round one begins, the training comes to fruition as these two highly talented fighters begin their match. To the surprise of many observers, the fight became one-sided, with Terence Crawford dominating Errol Spence. In the second round of the fight, Crawford lands a two-punch combination that sends Errol Spence to the canvas. Spence rises to his feet, but his legs appear to be unsteady. This is a bit surprising because it is so early in the fight. In the following rounds Crawford's dominance continues in an even more pronounced fashion. He repeatedly hurts Spence and knocks him down a total of three times during the fight. While Terence Crawford's focus, decision-making, big picture, and self-evaluation play a huge role in his dominance, Errol Spence's ability to keep getting up after each knock down is quite noteworthy. The fight continued until the ninth round. Spence did sustain tremendous punishment throughout those rounds. The aftermath of the fight resulted in Terence Crawford taking the titles not only physically but also becoming the best fighter in the world at this time.

Interestingly, the big conversation days after the fight is Errol Spence's ability to take a tremendous amount of punishment and continue to get up, only to endure more punishment. The fight ended with the referee stopping the contest. Spence finished on his feet after absorbing a tremendous amount of blows. Knockdowns in life and the boxing ring happen constantly, but the key lies in our ability to get up. Although Spence's performance was disappointing and the loss was devastating, the aftermath of the fight involved so much talk about his ability to take that punishment and continue to get up. Spence absorbed blow after blow repeatedly for nine rounds yet continued to fight. It's amazing to see how this was perceived by many in real time. The contrasting views concerning the fight are very interesting. Terence Crawford's performance solidified him as the world's number one fighter instead of Errol Spence's performance, raising questions about his abilities in the ring. Spence's performance allowed him to receive a prominent respect regarding his ability to weather the storm inside the ring and continue to fight. One more critical point to highlight around the results of this fight. Errol did look off pretty much from the start of the fight. Some observers believe he struggled to make the contracted weight of 147 pounds. Both boxers must weigh no more than 147 pounds for their matchup the day before the fight. Spence mentioned that he walks around at roughly 170 pounds when not training for a fight. Could that have been a factor in the fight? It is possible. However, when asked about this after the fight he made no excuses.

The legendary boxer-writer Dan Rafael, who covered the fight, stated his respect for Spence grew even more because he accepted the loss without making excuses. In the post-fight press conference, Rafael noted that Spence was allowed to make excuses. The media fed him excuses about weight, a swelling eye and inactivity in the ring. Each time Spence responded saying he was fine going into the ring, none of those things were a factor. This is a high level accepting "THE AGONY OF DEFEAT." Accepting that will allow Spence to prepare for a possible rematch between the boxers (at the time of this writing). Or maybe he will decide a rematch is not what he wants. Boxing is truly an analogy of life.

Accepting the thrill of victory and the agony of defeat is a critical part of our mental conditioning. It is profound because after all the work we put in to get to the point of determining the results, it is not a foregone conclusion that we understand the importance of accepting those results. Ironically, the intoxication of the thrill of victory sometimes makes it difficult to accept what it means in the scope of getting better as we move forward in our life's journey. When we gain the Mental Strength to understand all the training that goes into the "12 Rounds," including the reward of accepting the thrill of victory and agony of defeat results in:

YOU
BEING
THE
UNDISPUTED
CHAMPION
OF
LIFE!

CONCLUSION
POST-FIGHT INTERVIEW

After watching a hard-fought boxing matchup, it is always very intriguing and highly anticipated to hear what both fighters say in their interviews following the fight. Sometimes the verbal analysis of what happened is enlightening to those listening and the fighters themselves. Fighters get asked whether they felt their game plans were effective? Did they feel their conditioning was enough? We come full circle to those questions the fighters were asking themselves in Round 1 (deciding to get better) of this book. We experience this same line of questioning in our everyday lives. We go through many different fights with the opponent "LIFE." These fights are our journeys in life. We win some and we lose some. Regardless of the results, we must go through the post-fight interview with ourselves after each fight. It's a form of Self-Evaluation.

So, let's wrap up "12 Rounds of Mental Conditioning" by doing some post-fight questions!

Q – Which is the most important Principle of Mental Conditioning?

1 – Self-Evaluation.
2 – Decision Making.
3 – Big Picture.
4 – Staying the Course.

A – The importance of each principle varies depending on where you are in the fight against "LIFE." There will be times when the big picture will be most important. Other times, decision making will be most important. Sometimes, staying the course will prove to be most important. That said, we must evaluate where we are to determine which principle is most important at a given time. With that understanding, self-evaluation would have to be the most important principle of mental conditioning!

Q – Which Round of "12 Rounds Of Mental Conditioning" is the most significant?

A – Most similar to the principles, each round holds equal significance. The key factor is to understand which round you are in at a given time in your life. This is critical because if you believe you are in Round 10 (get up-grab and hold), but life is dictating you are in Round 9 (knockdown) you will have a severe problem pushing forward. This illustrates how important Self-Evaluation (Round 2) is in our fight against "LIFE."

Q – How Do You Know If You Won The Round?

A—Decision-making is key to our Mental Growth. As we start to enhance and sharpen our decision-making skills, it is a particularly good indication of us winning rounds. Formulating our big picture is a large part of establishing our path to success. When we achieve the goal of that big picture, it is also a clear indication of winning rounds.

Q – Is Mental Conditioning a replacement for therapy?

A—Mental Conditioning is not a replacement for therapy. Neither replaces the other. In fact, they complement each other. Although training our minds gives us the confidence to solve roadblocks in our lives, in some instances, we need outside help in the form of therapy. Therapy can bring out things we have difficulty bringing out ourselves. We still need to mentally train to perform our self-evaluations" to assess where we are as we make breakthroughs in our therapy.

Q – You obtained *the desired mental strength* you were looking for! What's next?

A – Return to the Mental Conditioning Gym and train some more. There is always a demand to get better. Remember the opponent called "LIFE" is in constant pursuit. There will always be another challenge to deplete the Mental Strength already built. Just like a World Champion in the Boxing Ring, we must continuously train to keep our minds sharp and keep the title "CHAMPION OF LIFE."

Thank you for going through these 12 Rounds with me. I will be sitting ringside to support everyone as we all swap mental punches with the " LIFE " opponent each day!!

www.ingramcontent.com/pod-product-compliance
Lightning Source LLC
Chambersburg PA
CBHW051247020426
42333CB00025B/3095